Editor

Jaroslava Gajdošíková Zeleiová

SPECTRUM SLOVAKIA Series
Volume 38

Quality of Life in Cross-Modal Perspectives of Inclusive Education

Bibliographic Information published by the Deutsche Nationalbibliothek
The Deutsche Nationalbibliothek lists this publication in the Deutsche Nationalbib-
liografie; detailed bibliographic data is available in the internet at http://dnb.d-nb.de.

Editor:
Jaroslava GAJDOŠÍKOVÁ ZELEIOVÁ

Reviewers:
Ladislav POŽÁR
Kateřina VITÁSKOVÁ

Translators:
Marina VIDANOVÁ
Eva KRÁLOVÁ

University of Trnava
Faculty of Education
Slovak Republic

Team of Authors:

Miroslava BARTOŇOVÁ	Chap 01
Naďa BIZOVÁ	Chap 04
Jaroslava G. ZELEIOVÁ	Chap 05
Grażyna GUNIA	Chap 07
Joanna KONARSKA	Chap 06
Viktor LECHTA	Chap 03
Annette LEONHARDT	Chap 08
Eva LÖRINCZOVÁ	Chap 02
Andrea PERLUSZ	Chap 09
Anna SÁDOVSKÁ	Chap 10
Marie VÍTKOVÁ	Chap 01
Erik ŽOVINEC	Chap 02

ISSN 2195-1845
ISBN 978-3-631-77439-7
Ebook: 978-3-631-78306-1
ePub: 978-3-631-78307-8
MOBI: 978-3-631-78308-5
DOI 10.3726/b15686
© Peter Lang GmbH
International Academic Publishers
Berlin 2022

ISBN 978-80-224-1721-1

© VEDA, Publishing House
of the Slovak Academy of Sciences
Bratislava 2022

This publication has been peer reviewed.

www.peterlang.com   www.veda.sav.sk

The monograph originated with the support of the Scientific Grant Agency of the Ministry of Education, Science, Research and Sport of the Slovak Republic and the Slovak Academy of Sciences No 1/0608/14 *Quality of life (for pupils with disabilities) in
Cross-modal Perspectives of Inclusive Education.*

Contents

Introduction

The European Disability Strategy (2010-2020): The renewed commitment to build Europe without barriers affects the course of events of individual European Union member states. The Council of Europe Action Plan
to promote the rights of people with disabilities and their full participation
in society: Improving the quality of life of people with disabilities in Europe in the years 2006-2015 has also affected transformative educational
efforts (action line 4 Education). However, the systematic implementation
of political decisions requires coordination of all the resorts, and in the
field of social school reforms, a thorough analysis of existing conditions is
required before social changes are made. The transformation of attitudes
and approaches towards the education of people with disabilities is not
possible without an indepth understanding school reality and the direct
impact of the inclusion made by political decisions on the quality of life of
all the persons involved in education.

The process of providing inclusive education is an integral part of the
education system (Policy Guidelines on Inclusion in Education. UNESCO,
2009, ED-2009/WS/31). Under this rule, which recommends to clearly specify an inclusive school policy, understood and accepted at the level of the
schools of common type, integrated education and local community programme are perceived as complementary approaches to the provision of
effective education. It is expected that the school community will use its
own resources, not excluding human potential. These policy guidelines,
however, will not be used without the cognition and elimination of the risks
and barriers of the creation of a functional school community.

The subject of this monograph is to analyse precisely the actual conditions of the education of children and young people with disabilities and
the assessment of the effectiveness and functionality of the schools that
have implemented inclusive education with the participation of those who
are directly affected by the system: pupils with disabilities, their parents,
school leavers and school staff. The ethical, social and professional dimension of inclusive pedagogy has a more significant transformational impact
on the quality of life of pupils with disabilities than the political aspects of
inclusion. However, they have not received proper attention.

Our purpose is to evaluate school and educational changes and analyse the interactions of persons involved in real-life education. That is why
the monograph aims to provide relevant and comparable data of the quality of life of pupils with disabilities in the context of various educational
approaches (integrated, specialized) in different cultural and economic
conditions of Central European countries. In individual studies, the authors identified specific limits and possibilities of the educational environ-

ment and its impact on the quality of life of children/pupils with disabilities (mental, sensory) or children with specific developmental learning disorders. Empirical data provide mapping of the actual implementation of the UN Convention on the Rights of Persons with Disabilities, particularly the article 24 of the Convention and the adherence to the Standard rules on equal opportunities for persons with disabilities (UNESCO, rule 6) in accordance with the UNESCO Policy Guidelines on Inclusion in Education in Central European countries.

The problems of every-age people with disabilities, disturbances, threats or disadvantages are determined by the dynamics of interactions between them and the social environment in which they live. Therefore, the bio-psycho-socio-spiritual model of health is globally linked to the civilian model, accentuating the active participation in the social life of a particular community. The interference and convergence of these models is present in the transdisciplinary theme of the publication, which examines the quality of life of pupils in inclusive education in the Central European region – in the V4 countries and German-Bavarian countries, where inclusive education has a different tradition.

We believe that the publication will approximate the evidence-based practice and enrich the competency-based approach by defining and applying supportive educational factors to the persons involved in education, their relatives and multidisciplinary school team. We hope that the monograph – in line with the call of the European agency for the development of education for people with special educational needs – will invite to address and update the educational inclusion as a complex of partial problems and possibilities in the practice itself.

Jaroslava Gajdošíková Zeleiová, editor

1 Mental Health as One of The Quality of Life Indicators

1.1 Introduction

In relation to joint or inclusion education of pupils at school, coping with mental health issues is the main area of concern (Heinold 2014). Inclusive education should meet the needs of both pupils in the classroom and their parents. The research shows a connection between the quality of teaching and the teacher effectiveness and between the mental health of teachers and pupils (Řehulka 2015, pp. 51–72).

1.2 Joint Education of Students in Inclusive School Environment

Inclusive teaching should address to the individual needs of pupils. Many factors can promote or prevent the development of an inclusive school. In one study from Israel, the factors that led to successful work practice in an inclusive school were collected (Biewer, Fasching 2012, p. 122). The most important factors were education and experience of teachers, relationship between teachers and pupils with special educational needs, graduation requirements for pupils with special educational needs (SEN) and readiness to support inclusion. For a successful teaching in the sense of inclusion, the following four criteria were required:

1. **Educational orientation:** Successful teachers are those who establish a relationship with their pupils that provided the pupils with courage and support. The teachers' knowledge about each pupil's personal needs and the teachers' contact with their parents are significant.
2. **Attitudes towards inclusion:** The widespread opinion was that all pupils with SEN should be educated in an inclusive school with the exception of pupils with severe disabilities and behavioural disorders.
3. **Practice in teaching:** Successful teachers should regularly discuss with their colleagues about teaching and educational problems.
4. **Personality traits:** Teachers should be sensitive to the pupils' needs; they should show their pupils affection and give them enough time. Their own success in teaching process is attributed to their competencies in teaching (teaching ability).

1.3 Psychological Well-Being as a Topic in Inclusive School

Mental health is an essential part of the concept of health. We can explain that as a successful interaction focused on the health topic (HT), according to Cohn (1975 in Langmack 2011). We assume that people feel well when they are healthy. People who are mentally healthy create *individual* (me), *interpersonal* (us) and *pragmatic relationships* (it) in a dynamic balance in their environment (Fig. 1). This is in agreement with the contemporary definition by Schaarschmidt and Kieschke (2007), who define mentally healthy people as the ones who face the demands of everyday life, follow their own goals, have a positive attitude towards themselves and towards their own behaviour, experience their activities in a meaningful way and feel socially integrated. Psychological well-being has roots in one's ability to find balance between self-preservation and self-formation (compare Paulus 2003) on personal, interpersonal and material levels, conditioned by environment, demands and needs. The dynamic balance emerges in a constant process of understanding, so one or more factors can be sometimes emphasized (Langmack 2011).

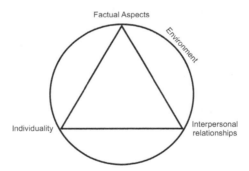

Fig. 1. Cohn Four Factor Model HT (1975 in Langmack 2011)

In inclusive schools, everyday life in terms of health interaction is influenced by demands and needs. All the participants at school encounter their individual needs, competencies and life stories, as well as curricular framework, spatial advantages and educational standards (compare Boban, Hinz 2003). To put dynamic balance into practice in a usual school day, it is necessary to try and to test how much it contributes to mental health at the four levels. A teacher can succeed when he or she answers the following questions:

- I: How can I maintain or restore my mental health? When do my pupils feel mentally healthy?
- We: How do I recognise that my class is mentally healthy, or that they act like mentally healthy? How can I support my class to stay or become mentally healthy?
- It: How can I apply the topic of mental health in educational process?
- Environment: How should I shape the classroom environment to provide for mental health and support it? How can understanding of mental health and associated factors contribute to a successful process?

1.4 Readiness of Children with SEN to Make Efforts during Classes

In schools, the learning process requires pupils to have competences and to use strategies. Pupils can self-regulate the goals they set; they are continuously forced under different conditions to decide whether to begin learning or not and to control their emotions. Students themselves check and realise the set objectives against their inner fear, remain under stress and are ready to command their efforts. Especially in a regular highly positive environment where learning is highly stimulated, a student must be able to make decisions in a relatively short time. It needs to be admitted that these competences are not significant for pupils with SEN. Pupils must turn back from the orientation to failure (Matthes 2006), and from the higher degree of fear or even from their own defence. The attributes of self-defence behaviour include, for example negative emotionality and tendency to withdraw. It is expected that the phase in which the pupils with SEN find themselves is shortened, so this seems to be only partial experience. Specifically, this means that pupils try quite a few things that prevent them from achieving their goals.

If pupils feel well in the inclusive environment of a school, it is the result of adaptation and regulatory processes (compare Becker 2003). The balance between inner and outer risks and protective factors for individual patterns of their adaption is required. Risk factors include special demands and needs of pupils with SEN that deter them from active performance; these risk factors act as a burden (compare Nerdinger, Blickle, Schaper 2008). On the other hand, protective factors are resources that help devise strategies through which pupils can overcome this burden.

Well-being can be reduced by the effects of risk factors or be strengthened by protective factors.

1.5 Risk Factors at School

Educational institutions have a great potential to influence social values and development. Promoting inclusive processes in schools can be seen as the necessary condition for building an inclusive and globalized society. Therefore, contemporary schools are exposed to the challenges of deep internal cultural changes. To control this transformation, good orientation of school leaders, not only in the field of inclusion but also in other areas related to the management and support of the people in schools, is required. To get inclusion into practice in schools is not always easy, especially in the context of the rapidly changing situation in the world, due to which the number of students gain voices highlighting the risks of mixing cultures and weakening the traditional values of local culture. Inclusion has today become entirely a political topic that – finally, like every political topic – has its enthusiastic supporters and a strong opposition too (Lazarová, Hloušková, Trnková, Pol, Lukas 2015).

Various research investigations in recent years have reported the internal and external stress factors for teachers and pupils (compare Hascher, Winkler-Ebner 2010; Schaarschmidt 2005; Schaarschmidt, Kieschke 2007). Teachers´ well-being is reduced by constantly introduced innovations in educational system, a lack of clear structures for their implementation, an increase in administrative duties and a large number of students in a classroom, among others. Pupils experience as a burden, for example missing possibility of co-decision, decommissioning, discrimination or violence. However, it should be noted that factors such as large classes, decommissioning or experience with discrimination are incompatible with inclusive environment of a successful school. Some inclusive conditions accordingly correspond with salutogenic culture, structures and practices. Other factors such as heterogeneity of a class or extracurricular duties are likely to be well received. What individually differs is how much they are perceived as burdensome.

A broad and balanced repertoire of strategies with protective factors is often lacking at schools. Risk factors prevail not only among students but also among teachers, and contribute to health hazard. The assessment of health of children and youth (compare Schlack, Kurth, Hölling 2008) indicates the proportion of mentally burdened children and youth in primary school and middle school (22.5%); 9.6% of them suffer from serious mental illnesses such as anxiety disorder, social behaviour, depression or attention-deficit/hyperactivity disorder (ADHD). The increased workload is more frequent among socially disadvantaged pupils. The research results (45%) indicate that the disproportionate demands on the teachers lead to their experiencing stress and overload, resulting in nervousness (Cihlars 2011). Schaarschmidt and Kieschke (2007) found that 28.7% teachers suffer from burnout syndrome. Similar data were obtained in a similar research in the Czech Republic (compare Řehulka 2015, pp. 51–72). When we consider that mentally healthy teachers and pupils are a prerequisite for the success of educational processes (Cihlars 2011; Hascher, Winkler-Ebner 2010), then the aforementioned burden has a negative impact on the quality of teaching and the teacher effectiveness.

1.6 Protective Factors at School

Zins et al. (2004) and Cihlars (2011) found that some protective factors that support wide interaction within the context of quality of teaching and school also support mental health. They advocate the strategies that help teachers manage activities and promote health, such as coherence (Nerdinger, Blickle, Schaper 2008). Firstly, teachers and pupils positively experience internal and external environment when they are structured, predictable and explainable. Strategies such as transparency in the regulation of responsibility, support of performance and feedback, and co-operation with extracurricular partners are required to foster a sense of clarity. Secondly, teachers and students should feel that they can handle the situation. For example, feeling of belongingness is addressed to experience social support. Confidence in their own abilities, as well as the development of a sense of self-worth, is seen as the result of recognition and success. And thirdly, involvement in a particular situation represents a challenge. A sense of purpose can be especially gained by careful behaviour towards colleagues in school management and leadership, mutual participation in school life and reinforcing the school connectedness. For pupils it is important to be reminded of the significance of life perspectives.

We can conclude that these protective factors are an essential part of inclusive cultures, structures and practices. Therefore, they foster psychological well-being in an inclusive school on individual, interpersonal and material levels, and help promote this in relation to environment. The resources such as participation and acceptance, respect for diversity and active shaping of school culture, could be the basis for successful establishment of salutogenic culture, structures and practices in a school (compare Lazarová, Hloušková, Trnková, Pol, Lukas 2015).

1.7 Mental Health and Inclusion – Strategies for the Development of Inclusive School

In order to maintain balance between self-preservation and self-fulfilment at school, it is necessary to systematically identify stressors in school at all levels and at the same time use school resources to promote mental health. The question is, what the main activity of school is, and how health aspect contributes to that (Brägger, Paulus, Posse 2005). HT may be involved in the development of high-quality teaching and of schools towards a good *healthy school*. In doing so, the school has the responsibility to promote mental health of partakers at school. The aim of a *good school* is, based on the requirements of education, fostering personal development of pupils (I) and the common life and work of all involved in the school (we). The primary task of a *healthy school* is to promote health and prevention strategies at school, as an integral part of the development of education as well as schools. Based on that school has to be developed by health education (it) and the appropriate framework conditions (environment). Basic tasks of healthy school and integral part of its development are health promotion and prevention. Using the qualitative framework IQES (*Instrumente für die Qualitätsentwicklung und Evalution in Schülen, Tools for the development of quality and evaluation in school*), schools can find the possibility to approach individual activities to a *good and healthy school* without losing sight of the whole school system (compare Brägger, Paulus, Posse 2005). If inclusion is understood as a (future) main activity of school, further tools (for example IQES) for the quality development of inclusive education and school must be taken into account. *Index for Inclusion*, presently the leading one, is developed using the subtitle *Steps to school for all* (Boban, Hinz 2003).

The theme IQES is consistent with *Inclusion Index*. It is clear that the additional costs for schools cannot be determined while dealing with the needs for good quality of education and the conditions for good learning. The comparison of both qualitative frameworks indicates two perspectives that were not noticed until present: the development of inclusive education and of school (Heinold 2014). The IQES topic *Role of school management* is not covered by indicators of *Index*. This is very unfortunate, because the school management has a vital impact on the schools (compare Schaarschmidt 2007). It is not included in the current *Index for inclusion*, as it is partly related to health and in order to permanently and effectively enhance the quality of education as of *healthy school*. However, mental health is an essential contributor to the realization of inclusive development processes. Schools that have joined to support salutogenic development of schools and education systematically implemented the strategies to cope with disabilities, so that the factors such as social environment do not affect education much. Coping with mental health of teachers and students therefore represents a substantial investment to create equal opportunities. In this way there can exist schools such as a "good healthy school" for all (Heinold 2014).

1.8 Pupils with SEN in Joint Education

The learning process of pupils with SEN is not possible without the understanding of conditions, support measures and implementation strategies in education. Education and social inclusion of pupils with SEN into school environment is influenced by many factors. Chiefly, it is necessary to take into account the personality traits of a student, as learning requires theoretical knowledge and practical experience of teachers. For efficient education, it is essential to select from the spectra of necessary support measures the ones that are most suitable in the present situation of a pupil. In the education of pupils with SEN, it is important to include the following aspects of education: the activities that improve movement and coordination, and focus on relaxation; the development of social interaction (self-understanding, stimulate interest in others, expressive arts, therapies); and the acquisition of basic knowledge and skills, as well as basic social rules (greetings, rules of conduct), moral education and ethics (compare Gajdoš, Baxová, Zíma 2012; Bartoňová 2014).

1.9 Research Study Presentation

In 2015–2016, we conducted a research with the goal to analyse how teachers approach to pupils with SEN in inclusive school environment (Hlavičková, Bartoňová, 2016). We searched the answers to the questions how the conditions for inclusive education in schools are set and how the teaching staff assess pupils with SEN. The survey was conducted as a part of a quantitative research in elementary schools in the district of Blansko (South Moravian Region). We interviewed 6 elementary schools, with inclusive education of pupils with SEN. The basic method used in the survey was a questionnaire answered by 38 teachers (76%). The questionnaire was a modification of questionnaire from the year 2014 (Bartoňová 2014).

Considering the scope of research, we introduced several partial research parameters. The most common branch of respondents' education was *Teacher training for the first grade of primary school* (25 teachers), 6 respondents studied the discipline of Special Education. Four respondents graduated *Teacher training for elementary school pupils* with 2 study branches (Biology and Chemistry, Arts and Music education, Czech Language and Arts, Mathematics and Biology) and 3 respondents abstained from answering questions. Primary schools that participated in our research had a certain number of pupils with SEN. Four teachers said that from 1 to 5 pupils with SEN study in their school; from 6 to 10 are inclusively educated pupils who have 5 respondents and 26 respondents said that 10 or more pupils with SEN study in their college; and 3 respondents abstained from answering questions.

Within the framework of defining categories of SEN in elementary schools, pupils with the following disabilities were included: mild mental disability (20), Down syndrome (15), physical disabilities (20), disrupted communication ability (15), specific learning disabilities (34), disorder behaviour (23), autism spectrum disorders (19), and multiple disabilities (7), as well as students with disabilities (6) and socially disadvantaged pupils (23). Auditory and visual impairment does not appear in any of the surveyed schools. We asked our respondents the following question: "What is the attitude of schools towards inclusive education?"

Research results show that the majority of schools apply the principles of inclusive education. Teachers co-operate, and school tries to provide adequate education for the pupils with SEN or to use appropriate tools. Negative answers were observed only in the first category, which deals with whether schools are competent to accept all pupils regardless of their

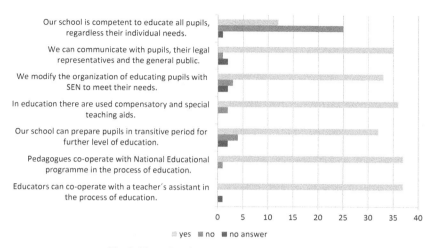

Fig. 2. The role of school in inclusive education

individual differences in the process of education. Twenty-five respondents believe that their school cannot educate all the students without discrimination. In the second category, the remarks of the two respondents indicated that although teachers can communicate, they unfortunately face reluctance or inability of communication from parents (Fig. 2).

Furthermore, we were interested in what approaches and which of supporting measures are perceived by teachers to be important and which ones are used in their educational practice (Figs. 3, 4).

The respondents answered questions using the following evaluation scale: *unimportant, more unimportant, more important,* and *very important.* The majority of respondents consider education in classroom with the least number of pupils, as well as use of visual aids, intensive revision of acquired knowledge and giving pupils enough time and space during their work, to be *very important.* Twenty-nine respondents consider positive student assessment and appraisal of their performance to be *very important.* The presence of two teachers in the classroom is perceived by 19 teachers as rather *unimportant,* education led by a special education teacher is perceived by 15 teachers as *unimportant* and inclusion of a special education subject is perceived similarly. Based on the views of the experts and our experience, however, we realize that the position of special education teacher and the establishment of special educational care unit are important steps towards a successful joint training.

All the respondents use the approach of frequent revision of gained knowledge in their work. They use visual aids, give pupils enough time to

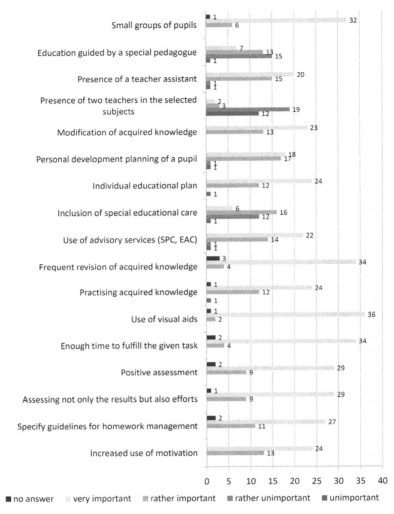

Fig. 3. Importance of approaches in education
Legend: SPC – Special pedagogical centre, EAC –Educational advisory centre

complete assigned tasks, use positive assessment and praise not only results but also efforts of pupils. In contrast, the approaches such as introducing subjects of special educational care into education, the lessons led by two teachers or a special education teacher and smaller groups are not used by the majority of our respondents. Why teachers do not use these approaches? We assume that the reason is that elementary school teachers have plenty of space for these approaches, and the overlapping of two

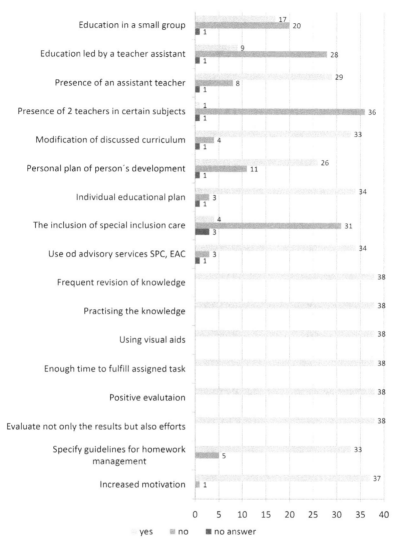

Fig. 4. Use of approaches in practice

teachers in one classroom (master's degree graduates) is supported by the new legislation (Decree No. 27/2016). As mentioned in the research study of Bartoňová (2014), the teaching staff utilizes the same teaching approaches during educational process.

Figure 5 illustrates the selected forms of teaching in joint education. Responses of respondents were recorded using an evaluation scale

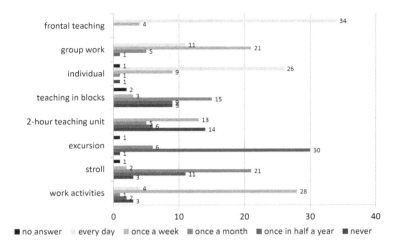

Fig. 5. Forms of school teaching

never, once in half a year, once a month, once a week, and *every day*. Most respondents identified the answer in all of the listed approaches. Figure 5 shows that 34 respondents (which is majority) used frontal teaching at work every day. By this type of teaching, teachers can transmit a greater amount of information to whole class in a relatively short time, and that suits them. Some research studies indicate that frontal teaching is one of the less appropriate forms of education for pupils with SEN, as it reduces their activity and does not allow them to develop adequately their independence and creativity and to rely on themselves. Individual teaching, which is based on a long-term working relationship between a student and a teacher, is considered a more appropriate form of education for pupils with SEN. The teacher approaches the student individually, respects his or her work pace and needs. Individual form of teaching is used by 26 (68%) respondents every day. Group work is another type of teaching that is recommended in inclusive education. Group work is used in everyday classes by 11 respondents, and 21 respondents use it once a week. Teaching in blocks is used once a month by 15 respondents, and it is used by 9 respondents once in half a year. Excursions are often not included in the educational process (30 respondents use them about once every 6 months). In ample amount work, activities are included in school classes, and 21 respondents included stroll in their school classes once a month. As suggested in the research study of Bartoňová (2014), the individual form of teaching and the use of active learning have been significantly increased, and the components of therapies continued to be implemented in primary schools.

If pupils with SEN are educated in inclusive school, appropriate conditions should be set, and these conditions should be observed at regular intervals and if necessary, they should be changed and modified. We were interested in how the respondents evaluate the success of inclusive education of pupils with SEN. The teachers used the following evaluation scale to express their answers: *absolutely unsuccessful, rather unsuccessful, half successful* and *very successful*. From the obtained answers, we concluded that inclusive education in the selected schools is generally successful education, although the majority of respondents' answers were *half successful* and they were unable to determine whether inclusive education is rather successful or rather unsuccessful. The efficiency in terms of acquired knowledge based on national educational programme was evaluated by 13 respondents as *rather successful*, 15 respondents evaluated it both successful and unsuccessful (*half-successful*) and only 2 respondents evaluated it as *absolutely unsuccessful*. The best-evaluated activity was the participation of pupils in teams, which was assessed by 4 respondents as *very successful*, 16 respondents evaluated it as *rather successful*, 12 respondents *half successful* and 4 respondents *rather unsuccessful*. In terms of acquiring necessary skills for life, 17 respondents evaluated the inclusion as *half-successful*, 11 teachers as *rather successful* and the rest of the respondents as *rather unsuccessful* or *absolutely unsuccessful*. The aspect of further education is evaluated by 16 respondents as *half successful* and by 9 teachers as *rather successful*, 8 as *rather unsuccessful* and 3 as *absolutely unsuccessful*. Choice of secondary school for pupils with SEN was evaluated by 7 respondents as *rather successful*, 15 as *half-successful*, 11 as *rather unsuccessful* and 3 as *absolutely unsuccessful*. The involvement of pupils in class team is at a better level than it was in the research study of Bartoňová (2014).

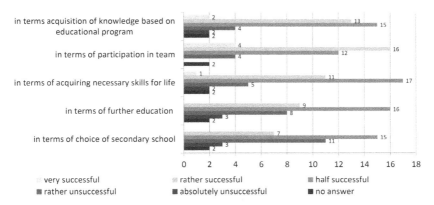

Fig. 6. Successfulness of inclusive education

Conversely, acquiring skills that are important in the lives of students was not as successful as teachers reported 2 years ago (Fig. 6).

Another question was directed towards the specification of improvement in inclusive education.

The results show that the majority of respondents need assistance in all areas, except the area where there should be the concurrence of two teachers in classes: a special education teacher and a teacher of primary school. Of the total respondents, 24 respondents (63%) are not identified with the impact of parallel teaching of two teachers. However, parallel teaching of two teachers is one of the essential features of inclusion. This situation confirms the hypothesis that teachers are concerned about the presence of another teacher in the classroom, but this concern (based on the interviews with teachers) is often the consequence of lack of their experience. Thirty-seven respondents (97%) would be happy if they had more financial resources for schools. Some of them rather highlighted this form of help, which is quite expected. Thirty respondents consider the establishment of the position of school special educator to be important, and only 7 respondents disagree. Twenty-four respondents would be happy with the establishment of a school position of a school psychologist. Most of the surveyed teachers welcomed more didactic and teaching tools for pupils; they participated in trainings and seminars that focus on inclusive education and welcomed regular consultations with experts who have direct experience and are oriented in the field of special education (Fig. 7).

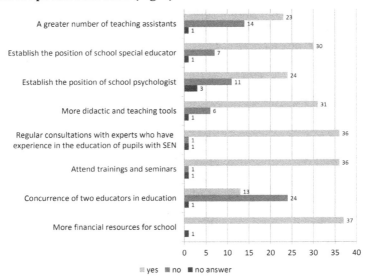

Fig. 7. Help in the education of pupils with SEN

The respondents were further asked to give their opinion on the indicators that affect inclusive education.

Several factors were selected to which the respondents answered *yes* and *no*. For this question, there were only two negative responses. One of the respondents did not consider the recognition of the individual student's needs in the inclusive class to be an important issue, and it was also specified that inclusion did not affect the teamwork of educators. All respondents agreed that in inclusive classes the following features were important: lower class sizes, positive school climate, individual approach to each student, intensive cooperation with the family and the use of appropriate technical and didactic aids (Fig. 8).

What difficulties do teachers have with the implementation of inclusive education?

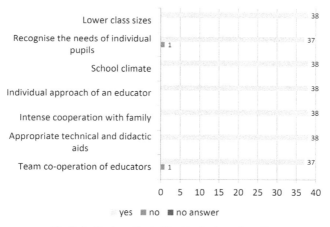

Fig. 8. Indicators that affect inclusive education

The inclusion is currently being the most debated topic, and therefore, we were interested what caused the teachers to fail in inclusive education. The semi-closed questions, where in the last question called *another,* the respondents could supplement their notes. This option was used only by two surveyed teachers. As an example of barriers of inclusive education, teachers said that not all pupils with SEN desire to be integrated into mainstream classes and they can experience success and do not fail as often in their natural environment. Completely different needs of pupils are described in lower mentioned example.

The respondents selected *yes* and *no* answers and were allowed to choose more answers; teachers circled 5 replies in average. Figure 9 shows that all 38 respondents agreed that a big barrier to inclusive education is too much pressure from the state to make rapid changes in the current system, which was emphasised by some respondents in the questionnaire by adding lots of exclamation marks or by retaining it. Thirty-seven respondents considered a large number of pupils in classes to be an obstacle, and 35 respondents mentioned a lack of financial resources of the schools. Twenty respondents felt insufficiently prepared for inclusive education. Only 6 teachers said that they did not have enough opportunities to educate pupils in the field of inclusion, and 24 respondents indicated that the schools lacked teaching assistants. However, the majority of surveyed respondents did not consider insufficient support of consultancy services, negative attitudes of parents towards inclusive education, parents' unwillingness to co-operate with school or teachers' unwillingness to work beyond their duties to be an obstacle for inclusive education. In addition, 25 respondents did not consider plenty of or lack of educational materials and methodologies concerning inclusive education to be a barrier (Fig. 9).

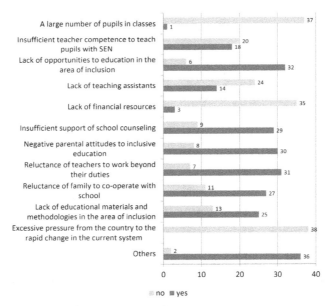

Fig. 9. Difficulties of inclusive education

1.10 Research Conclusions

Based on the research conducted, we can conclude that selected elementary schools include pupils with SEN, but the schools are still not adequately prepared to educate all the pupils based on their special needs. These schools mainly have pupils with mild forms of SEN; none of the teachers has the experience of teaching pupils with hearing or visual impairment. Teachers use the opportunity to co-operate with a school counsellor employed at their school, with the frequency of meeting him or her once a month. At least once a week, teachers exchange their experience with the colleagues at school and ask them for advice. They co-operatively consult with them about educational problems of pupils with SEN. They seek to form a stable unified team for teaching pupils with SEN. Especially colleagues at school are considered one of the most important participants in terms of co-operation in inclusive education. The majority of teachers in the classroom also collaborate with the teacher's assistant, whose task is determined by the support measures required for pupils with SEN. An assistant teacher is considered as the most important subject in terms of co-operation. They can communicate with legal representatives of the pupils and try to work with them, even though it is sometimes impossible for their parents. During classes, teachers apply support measures and use all the available compensatory and special teaching aids. Most of them use literary devices, computers and pictorial material. Primary schools try at the most to adapt education to pupils with SEN so that it would correspond to their true capabilities. They try hard to provide education at the highest possible level. In spite of, schools complain of deficiencies. Among them are mere negative attitudes of teachers that inclusion is not good or beneficial. Another deficiency is the concern of some teachers to appoint a special education teacher and a school psychologist. Educators are also aware of the fact that they are not ready for two pedagogues – a primary school teacher and a special education teacher.

It is necessary for the teachers of pupils with SEN to be educated in the field of special education if they really want to be good teachers. The research suggests that not all the surveyed teachers have special education training and some are not even interested in its completion. Teachers often prefer frontal instruction to individual or individualised instruction. It can be considered a positive that they use elements of alternative forms of education (for example learning by doing). All schools face a major problem over which they have no control. The problem lies in the lack of financial resources, which are the must for a high-quality education and inclusion. Research data show that teachers evaluate inclusive education of pupils with SEN as *rather successful*. The involvement of pupils with SEN in the class group is usually carried out without difficulties and does not disturb class environment in any way. The other pupils in the class are explained the specifics of the pupil with SEN, the resultant approaches and the method of evaluation. Pupils usually master the acquisition of knowledge according to the relevant educational programme with minor difficulties.

1.11 Conclusion

Pupils with SEN are unique in their specifics, each of them is an individual personality, and they need greater individual approach and respect for their true potential. Teachers are aware that it is necessary to use support measures that help maximize their efficiency in education of pupils with SEN. In classes, teachers can apply different approaches and methods, whichever they prefer. Teachers often repeat and practice what they had already learned, add teaching examples with visual aids and support the process of easier remembering in pupils. Teachers give pupils enough time to complete the assigned task and more frequently try to use elements for motivating and stimulating the attention and activity of pupils. Teachers appreciate not only results but also efforts of the pupils during the assessment. By positive motivation of pupils to do other activities, teachers try to evaluate each pupil's progress. To balance developmental inequalities among pupils, teachers create personal developmental plan for a pupil. Some teachers rather use different approach. They try to alternate activities regularly and include relaxation during classes as well as to avoid overburdening pupils. They strive for the best possible level of processing of received information by exploiting multiple channels of pupils when they receive information and highlight it to the greatest possible extent.

The research results show that pupils in inclusive classroom get on better in cognitive and social learning; there is no teaching or support that could not be implemented in a mainstream school. Inclusive teaching means better use of resources. Inclusion is socially inevitable; all pupils need a teacher that can teach them how to start relationships, how to maintain relationships and how to work with others. Inclusion reduces fears, and finally promotes friendship, respect and understanding. To maintain inclusive school environment and provide inclusive teaching, heterogeneous age grouping was proven as the best way. Heterogeneous age groupings allow teachers to easily accept the diversity of pupils and refrain from traditional ways. Age heterogeneity in a group enables students become more tolerant and willing to help their classmates. In such an environment it is obvious that everyone does something else, so there does exist no direct comparison of performance, and hence no rivalry. Each one is recognized for what he or she is in reality.

Literature

BARTOŇOVÁ, M. *Inkluzivní didaktika v základní škole se zřetelem na edukaci žáků s lehkým mentálním postižením.* 1. dotisk 1. vyd. Brno, MU, 2014, 224 p. ISBN 978 80-210-6560-4.

BECKER, P. Anforderungs-Ressourcen-Modell in der Gesundheitsförderung. In FRANCKOVIAK, P. (ed.). *Leitbegriffe der Gesundheitsförderung. Glossar zu Konzepten Strategie und Methoden in der Gesundheitsförderung.* Schwabenheim a. d. Selz: Sabo, 2003, pp. 13–15. ISBN 978-3-927916-16-6.

BIEWER, G. – FASCHING, H. Von der Förderschule zum inklusiven Bildungssystem – die Perspektive der Schulentwicklung. In HEIMLICH, U. – KAHLERT, J. (eds.). *Inklusion in Schule und Unterricht.* Wege zur Bildung für alle. Stuttgart: Kohlhammer, 2012, pp. 117–152. ISBN 978-3-17-025725-2.

BOBAN, I. – HINZ, A. *Index für Inklusion – Lernen und Teilhabe in der Schule der Vielfalt entwickeln.* Online. 2003, p. 123. Dostupné na: http://www.eenet.org.uk/resources/docs/Index%20German.pdf.

BRÄGGER, G. – PAULUS, P. – POSSE, P. *Gute gesunde Schule.* Definition Sigriswil September. Online. 2005. Verfügbar unter: http://www.anschub.de/cps/rde/xchg/ SID-0A000F0A-62CC8A34/anschub/hs.xsl/die_ziele.htm.

CIHLARS, D. *Die Förderung der Berufszufriedenheit von Lehrkräften. Individuelle, soziale und organisationsbezogene Maßnahmen der schulischen Personalentwicklung.* Bad Heilbrunn: Klinkhardt Forschung, 2011. ISBN 978-3-7815-1838-4.

GAJDOŠ, A. – BAXOVÁ, P. – ZÍMA, V. *Model inkluzivního vzdělávání v* ČR. Závěrečná zpráva z *výzkumu.* Praha: Rytmus s.r.o., 2012. Dostupné na: http://www.rytmus.org/download/zprava.pdf.

HASCHER, T. – WINKLER-EBNER, C. Gesundheit und Bildung von Kindern und Jugendlichen. In PAULUS, P. (ed.). *Bildungsförderung durch Gesundheit Bestandsaufnahme und Perspektiven für eine gute gesunde Schule.* Weinheim: Juventa, 2010, pp. 31–56.

HEINOLD, F. Inklusion beginnt im Kopf – Als gute gesunde Schule eine Schule für ALLE schaffen? In SCHUPPENER, S. (ed.). *Inclusion und Chancengleichheit. Diversity im Spiegel von Bildung und Didaktik.* Bad Heilbrunn: Verlag Julius Klinkhardt, 2014, pp. 117–123. ISBN 978-3-7815-1962-6.

HLAVIČKOVÁ, A. *Přístupy pedagogů k žákům se speciálními vzdělávacími potřebami v inkluzivní škole.* Diplomová práce. Brno: MU, 2016.

ICF. *Internationale Klassifikation der Funktionsfähigkeit, Behinderung und Gesundheit.* Genf: WHO, 2005. Dostupné na: http://www.soziale-initiative.net/wp-content/uploads/2013/09/icf_endfassung-2005-10-01.pdf.

ICF-CY. *Internationale Klassifikation der Funktionsfähigkeit, Behinderung und Gesundheit bei Kindern und Jugendlichen.* Bern: Verlag Hans Huber, 2011.

LANGMACK, B. *Einführung in die Themenzentrierte Interaktion (TZI). Das Leiten von Lern- und Arbeitsgruppen erklärt und praktisch angewandt.* Weinheim, Basel: Beltz, 2011. ISBN 978-3-407-22921-2.

LAZAROVÁ, B. – HLOUŠKOVÁ, L. – TRNKOVÁ, K. – POL, M. – LUKAS, J. *Řízení inkluze ve škole.* Brno: MU, 2015, preprint.

MATTHES, G. *Individuelle Lernförderung bei Lernstörungen.* Stuttgart: Kohlhammer, 2009. ISBN 978-3-17-020531-4.

NERDINGER, F. W. – BLICKLE, G. – SCHAPER, N. *Arbeits- und Organisationspsychologie.* Berlin, Heidelberg: Springer Medizin, 2008. ISBN 978-3-642-16972-4.

PAULUS, P. Psychologieunterricht und psychische Gesundheit. *Psychologie Unterricht,* 2003, 36, pp. 10–20.

ŘEHULKA, E. Psychologické otázky vzdělávání žáků se speciálními vzdělávacími potřebami v základní škole. In BARTOŇOVÁ, M. – VÍTKOVÁ, M. (eds.). *Vzdělávání se zaměřením na inkluzivní didaktiku a vyučování žáků se speciálními vzdělávacími potřebami ve škole hlavního vzdělávacího proudu.* Brno: MU, 2013, pp. 45–58. ISBN 978-80-210-6678-6.

ŘEHULKA, E. Psychologické a psychohygienické otázky vzdělávání žáků se zdravotním postižením z pohledu inkluze. In OŠLEJŠKOVÁ, H. – VÍTKOVÁ, M. et al. (eds.). *Východiska, podmínky a strategie ve vzdělávání žáků s těžkým postižením na základní škole speciální.* Brno: MU, 2014, pp. 39–54. ISBN 978-80-210-6673-1.

ŘEHULKA, E. Inkluzivní vzdělávání a osobnost učitele. In BARTOŇOVÁ, M. – VÍTKOVÁ, M. (eds.). *Inkluze ve škole a ve společnosti jako interdisciplinární téma.* Brno: MU, 2015, pp. 51–72. ISBN 978-80-210-8093-5.

SCHAARSCHMIDT, U. – KIESCHKE, U. *Gerüstet für den Schulalltag. Psychologische Unterstützungsangebote für Lehrerinnen und Lehrer.* Weinheim, Basel: Beltz, 2007. ISBN 978-3-407-25465-8.

SCHLACK, R. – KURTH, B. M. – HÖLLING, H. Die Gesundheit von Kindern und Jugendlichen in Deutschland. In *Umweltmedizin in Forschung und Praxis, Schwerpunkt Schule. Gesundheit von Kindern und Jugendlichen in Deutschland.* 2008, 13 (4), pp. 245–260.

VÍTKOVÁ, M. Mezinárodní klasifikace funkčních schopností, disability a zdraví. In OŠLEJŠKOVÁ, H. – VÍTKOVÁ, M. et al. (eds.) *Východiska, podmínky a strategie ve vzdělávání žáků s těžkým postižením na základní škole speciální.* Brno: MU, 2013, pp. 31–38. ISBN 978-80-210-6673-1.

ZINS, J. E. et al. The scientific base linking social and emotional learning to school access. In *Building Academic Success on Social and Emotional Learning. What Does the Research Say?* Part I. New York: Teacher College Press, 2004. ISBN 0-8077-4436-5.

2 Social Skills and Inclusion

2.1 Introduction

Educating pupils with specific learning disabilities (SLD) in inclusion classes is an important objective of educational policies in various countries. Dimension of social inclusion was examined by Koster, Nakken, Pijl and Van Houten (2009) who distinguished and described the dimension of social inclusion in three overarching concepts: social participation, interaction with people in school settings and social inclusion. Social skills represent the ability to interact with others either verbally or non-verbally (body language). We know that students´ behaviour is influenced by a range of factors. Among the most important are family and school environment, because the non-disabled pupils and pupils with SLD are in the process of social learning. Various research studies (for example Chien, Harbin 2012; Guzman, Caal 2014) draw the reader's attention to social and emotional learning, and they seek ways to implement them effectively in inclusive classroom and family environment. Social skills and behavioural problems of students with SLD (primary and secondary symptomatology) are the most common argument against the implementation of full inclusive educational policy and reconstruction of special education.

2.2 Family and Development of Social Skills

Many parents agree with the inclusion policy, and the number of students with special needs is increasing from year to year in mainstream schools (mainstreaming is the practice of educating students with special needs in regular classes during specific time periods based on their skills). The main advantage of inclusive education is that it provides not only academic benefits, but also positive benefits of socialization (Frederickson, Dunsmuir, Lang, Monsena 2004). This system provides an opportunity for a child to develop a positive relationship with his or her peers and to be integrated into social life (Scheepstra, Nakken, Pijl 1999). However, international studies have repeatedly shown that the inclusion of pupils with special needs, specifically pupils with SLD, does not automatically lead to increased friendship among the pupils and their peers (Buysse, Davis Goldman, Skinner 2002; Guralnick, Neville, Hammond, Connor 2007).

Relationships within families are considered very significant. However, the research studies vary in this aspect. McKeown and Pratschke a Haase (2003) virtually did not find any statistically significant differences in the development of pupils in four types of families. This suggests that the marital status of parents and the presence of one or two parents in the household do not necessarily affect the welfare of a child. The existing evidence of how different types of families can affect children suggests that the nature of home environment is not the most important factor. The quality of relationships and family economic background are of primary importance (Hobcraft, Kiernan 2001). A higher percentage of single parents children in household may activate inadaptability or emotional problems, in comparison to the children who live with both parents. This is probably due to economic status, not due to parental marital status.

We consider parental conflicts to be an important indicator of a child's emotional problems, mainly the ones directly concerning children, thereby increasing the lack of life chances for children. McKeown et al. (2003) found that life satisfaction of children is affected by the very first processes, which are thus considered the most important ones. These are for example unresolved problems between a child and his or her parents, including conflicts relating to behaviour (for example homework, school progress); family problems (for example doing things for family, routine communication); and personal autonomy (for example the responsibility of a child for his or her behaviour).

Often the problem lies in mutual communication between a parent and a child. Communication with parents is even more important for children with certain disabilities. Rothbauer (2008) asks the basic question, which is very important in communication, *"Can my child really listen?"* The basic prerequisite for effective communication is to recognize that children of all ages will, naturally and honestly, rather talk to their parents who know them well. Parents, however, often react differently than what their children expect, or they do not listen carefully or pretend to have all the answers immediately. These, however, would block the communication with a child and would function in an opposite way as parents expect. There are several strategies of how to support an effective communication. Firstly, it is important for parents to reformulate the sentence of what their child said in their own words. This gesture implies that they not only listen but also understand the message. Very important is also non-verbal communication such as facial expressions and body language of the child that should not be overlooked by parents as well. In this case, the rule is that the body language never lies. Parents should also control their child's tone of voice and be able to react adequately. Finally, yet importantly is the use of encouraging words that support the interest of parents in the conversation (for example *"Really ..."*, *"... then what happened?"*) (Rothbauer 2008). A lot of pressure is put on parents of children with particular disability, and every parent wants only the best for their children. Herényiová and Gajdošová (2002) believe that many parents are not well prepared for the role of educators of their children. They fall into extremes in the process of education, because they select either too authoritarian parenting style or too lax, benevolent and spilling education. Parents do not realize that insufficiently traced boundaries can cause many problems and hardship in educational relationships. Rogge (2007) claims that: *"... Children need boundaries, as early as possible, when we want to raise them to independence and autonomy. Without independence and autonomy, they will not be able to perceive his/her own self-worth, self-identity, confidence in ones' own potencial and strength is also not possible, nor courage to face challenges."* In this case, we talk about social skills that have an important and irreplaceable significance and play an important role in family environment.

2.3 Social Skills and Their Impact on Participation of Pupils with Special Educational Needs

Ten- to fifteen-year-old children and pupils need to be a part of certain community, to belong somewhere, to be popular and to have friends. In this age, there is an increased need for friendship and intimacy. The influence of peer group prevails over the influence of adults, including parents. Thus, school environment represents the best opportunity for new relationships and friendships. On the other hand, social exclusion in school environment can lead to complete isolation in social life. The lack of social contact with friends, low ability to control social skills and negative self-image can lead to the problems that can be demonstrated by aggressive behaviour (Cambra, Silvestre 2003).

Just, Pavri, and Luftig (2000) point out the fact that the inclusive educational tracking of pupils with SLD in the compulsory schools does not guarantee their acceptance in social dimension and positive social development. The authors report that pupils with SLD feel loneliness more than their peers do and they are less popular and more controversial in their social status. In addition, they do not participate in joint activities, which reflect a lack of their social skills. Guralnick et al. (2006) consider social skills necessary for social, emotional and personal development of pupils who are largely influenced by complex interrelation.

Within this context, the focus should be on social skills, which can be considered a predictor of high-quality relationships, also in school environment. Elliott et al. (2001) define the social skills as skills that facilitate starting and maintaining positive social relationships, contribute to peer acceptance and development of friendship and finally allow individuals to cope and adapt to the demands of social environment. Gresham and Elliott (1990) focus on the skill of co-operation that is important in helping and respecting classmates and others, and in following the rules. Furthermore, they focus on the skill of assertiveness, which is considered a proactive behaviour, the ability to be able to ask others for information, to promote one's own personality without conflictand to respond to others in an appropriate way. Finally, they focus on the skill of empathy that leads to take up interest in and respect for the feelings and opinions of the others and is the ability to listen actively and empathize with the feelings of one's classmates and peers. Goleman (1995) says that empathy means to be interested in other people and understand their emotions, or the ability to see the situation from their point of view.

Elliott et al. (2001) consider these social skills to be important for the successful socialization and academic success of all students. They are also significant in the prevention of negative evaluation by the others, and therefore are considered important aspects of efficient schools. Social skills may be developed at different levels in individual students. While one pupil tolerates the others in his or her class, is able to make friends, and listens to others, another pupil may appear as a loner, or possibly does not know how to establish common communication. We must eliminate such differences in school environment in order to avoid conflicts in the classroom, aggressive behaviour or social exclusion. Social skills can be understood through the skills that we use to communicate and interact with other people in society (Patrick 2011). They are based on the social norms of our society and tell us what behaviour and attitudes are considered acceptable in certain social situations. They are also important because they allow us to communicate with a certain predictability to each other and thus we can understand each other much better. Students with developed social skills are considered capable and successful. The majority is like them, while pupils without social skills are considered unfit. Therefore, failure in learning social skills can lead to isolation, loneliness, frustration, feelings of rejection and low self-esteem. Kročanová (2012) considers them the key factors that determine the success of social integration. Social skills have an impact on how a child is accepted by his or her peers, how they treat and respect him or her. The author focuses her research mainly on hearing impaired children, but we believe that even in other types of disabilities social skills play a key role in the participation of students in a social group. The results of the study of Zbortekova (2012) suggest that disabled pupils are repeatedly confronted with loneliness, indifference or even rejection in everyday contact with their non-disabled peers.

2.4 Research Study Presentation

Lack of social support is perceived as a serious problem that can complicate the formation of individual identity. Therefore, we should focus primarily on the development of social skills, both in pupils with SLD and in non-disabled ones. The elimination of big differences in social skills of these pupils could lead to active social inclusion, good cooperation and mutual understanding.

We continue with the assessment of social skills of both pupils with SLD and non-disabled ones in mainstream schools. Referring to the aforementioned, we draw our attention to the social skills of co-operation, assertiveness and empathy in school environment. The aim of our research is to examine for which variables (assertiveness, empathy, co-operation) are students not statistically different.

2.5 Research Sample

Research sample consisted of 105 respondents – pupils of 9th grade aged from 14 to 15 years, who studied in lower secondary schools. We consider the selection of 9th graders to be the most efficient, because the pupils are in a transition period of attending high school. We can conclude that they are ready to adapt to new environment of continuing education in terms of social skills. Of 105 respondents, 44 (42%) were boys and 61 (58%) girls. Respondents were divided into two groups: non-disabled pupils (83; 79%) and pupils with SLD (22; 21%). The research sample consisted of pupils from common Slovak elementary schools in Nitra and Košice. The research was conducted in the period between October 2015 and November 2015.

2.6 Methods

Social Skills Rating System–Student Forms (SSRS; Gresham, Elliott 1990) is the instrument designed for assessing several personal characteristics. We adapted the items to the entries suitable for 14- and 15-year-olds, and then we compiled and modified the range of social skills that consisted of 3 subscales: *Cooperation, Assertiveness* and *Empathy.* Particular subscales consisted of 4 items for *Cooperation, Assertiveness* and 5 items for *Empathy.* The reliability of instrument was measured by Cronbach's alpha coefficient and was satisfactory (M = 0.740).

2.7 Results and Discussion

In Table 1, descriptive data of the intensity of individual variables in the research sample are presented. Almost all variables range over an arithmetic average (for the variables of *Cooperation* and *Assertiveness* M = 12.00; and for the variable *Empathy* M = 15).

Tab. 1. Descriptive Statistics of Research Data

Factor	N	M	SD	SEM	Min	Max	SK	KU
Cooperation	105	15.10	2.51	0.25	5	20	-0.64	1.51
Assertiveness	105	14.26	3.16	0.31	4	20	-0.54	0.65
Empathy	105	18.20	3.30	0.32	10	25	-0.25	-0.36

Legend: N-number; M-mean; SD-standard deviation; SEM-standard error of measurement; Min-a minimum score acquired in a relevant group; Max-a maximum score acquired in relevant group; SK-asymmetric division; KU-kurtosis of a data set.

For evaluating social skills at the level of individual subscales of SSRS in non-disabled pupils and pupils with SLD, we calculated statistically significant difference in the variable *Empathy* (F = 2.099, p = 0.038) at the level of 0.05 (Table 2).

Non-disabled pupils had a significantly higher mean score of 1.63 points compared to pupils with SLD. Non-disabled pupils also had higher mean scores at the level of other variables of SSRS questionnaire (in the variable *Cooperation*, 0.07 points, and in the variable *Assertiveness*, 1.41 points). However, these differences were not statistically significant. Figure 1 shows the differences between research groups in the variables.

Tab. 2. Differences in the Variables of Scale SRSS in Intact Pupils and in Pupils with SLD

Variable	Group	N	M	SD	Df	t	p
Cooperation	INT	83	15.12	2.510	103	0.124	0.902
	LD	22	15.5	2.572			
Assertiveness	INT	83	14.55	3.077	103	1.893	0.061
	LD	22	13.14	3.299			
Empathy	INT	83	18.54	3.314	103	2.099	0.038
	LD	22	16.91	2.959			

Legend: INT-Non-disabled pupils; LD-(according to present School Act) pupils with learning disabilities; N-number; M-mean; SD-standard deviation; Df-degrees of freedom; t-Student's t-test; p-level of statistical significance.

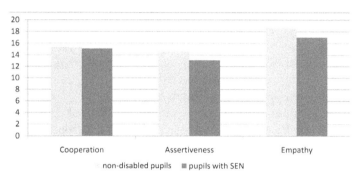

Fig. 1. Differences in the Variables of Questionnaire SRSS in non-disabled Pupils and in Pupils with SLD (SEN)

2.8 Conclusion

We focused on the social skills of both groups, non-disabled pupils and pupils with SLD, from mainstream school. The differences in mean were observed for the variables *Cooperation* (0.07 point) and *Assertiveness* (1.41 points), but statistically significant difference was shown for the variable *Empathy* (F = 2.099, p = 0.038) at the level of 0.05 (Table 2). The results of the study (Frostad, Pijl 2007) also point to the fact that the non-disabled pupils achieved better values of social skills than their classmates with SLD. We believe that the variable *Empathy* points to an important problem in the school environment that needs to be dealt with. In class, this may cause unsatisfactory communication or assertiveness towards pupils with SLD. We also believe that these pupils do not want to be in the spotlight, and for this reason, they prefer privacy and do not express their opinions and attitudes in the classroom. Many research studies (Bryan, Bryan 1990; Kavale, Forness 1996; LaGreca, Vaughn 1992) focus on the pupils with SLD who have lower degree of social skills, which they associate with insufficient establishment of relationships among group members. This is closely related to the research of Trlicová (1995); (hearing impairment) and Učeň (2002), who point to the low social status of students with special needs in a common school environment.

An emphasis should be placed on developing social skills, for example by their training. It is important to develop and maintain contacts, relationships and friendships among peers to eliminate social exclusion, aggressive behaviour or low self-image. Jordán et al. (1991) say that the programmes for the development of social skills support healthy spiritual and social development. They are based on the social and emotional aspects that refer to a basis of social skills aimed at helping students to cope with many challenges in their lives (Elias 1995). They are designed to provide safe and cooperative environment in the classroom orientated to intellectual, social and emotional development of students.

Programmes aimed at the development of social skills also highlight elimination of insufficient and aggressive behaviour (Grossman et al. 1997); improvement of social adaptation, peer relationships (Battistich 2003); and expression of one's own emotions (Greenberg et al. 1995).

Therefore, we should not forget how important is to develop the skills of parents that they need in upbringing of their children. As mentioned above, the overall participation is affected not only by school environment, but also by family environment and the quality of relationships between family members. Social skills lead to significant changes in the behaviour of parents and children themselves. For example, one of the studies (Bradley, Hayes 2007) suggests that parents can reduce the aggressive symptoms of the child from 20% to 60%. Parents as well as their children learn skills that are aimed at co-operation, effective communication, problem-solving and empathic expression. It is equally important for parents to be able to anticipate events and promote positive interaction with their child. Those parents who provide proper discipline and draw attention to the overall behaviour of their children, in a certain way, promote the involvement of children with their peers, thus enable them to take responsibility for their behaviour, and they teach them how to critically evaluate critical situation. If parents show empathy towards their children and support them in expressing their own emotions (especially the negative ones), their children will have greater social skills (Roberts, Strayer 1996), higher sociometric status and better friendships (McElwain, Halberstadt, Volling 2007), while they will also display a greater tendency to empathy and prosocial behaviour (Zahn-Waxler 1991).

We consider social skills to be an important component for pupils' further studies and of their lives. We believe disabled pupils and special pupils with SLD will have a number of social related problems that their family and school should get prepared for. Therefore, it is necessary to pay more attention to social skills, not only in special educational concept of intervention but also in a preventive sense of focusing on all students.

Literature

BATTISTICH, V.: Effects of a school-based program to enhance prosocial development on children's peer relations and social adjustment. *Journal of Research in Character Education.* 2003, 1 (1), pp. 1–17.

BRADLEY, S. – HAYES, N.: Children with behavioural problems. *Centre for Social & Educational Research.* 2007.

BUYSSE, V. – DAVIS GOLDMAN, B. – SKINNER, M. L.: Setting effects on friendship formation among young children with and without disabilities. *Exceptional Children.* 2002, 68, pp. 503–517.

CAMBRA, C., SILVESTRE, N.: Students with special educational needs in the inclusive classroom: Social integration and self-concept. *European Journal of Special Needs Education.* 2003, 18, pp. 197–208.

CHIEN, N., HARBIN, V.: Encouraging the development of key life skills in elementary school-age children: A literature review and recommendations to the Tauck Family Foundation Washington. *Child Trends.* 2012.

ELIAS, M. J.: Primary prevention as health and social competence promotion. *Journal of Primary Prevention.* 1995, 16 (1), pp. 5–24.

ELLIOTT, S. N. – MALECKI, CH. K. – DEMARAY, M. K.: New directions in social skills assessment and intervention for elementary and middle school students. *Exceptionality: A Special Education Journal.* 2001, 9 (1–2), pp. 19–32.

FREDERICKSON, N. – DUNSMUIR, S. – LANG, J. – MONSEN, J. J.: Mainstream-special school inclusion partnerships: Pupil, parent and teacher perspectives. *International Journal of Inclusive Education.* 2004, 8, pp. 37–57.

FROSTAD, P. – PIJL, S. J.: Does being friendly help in making friends? The relation between the social position and social skills of pupils with special needs in mainstream education. *European Journal of Special Needs Education.* 2007, 22, pp. 15–30.

GAJDOŠOVÁ, E. – HERÉNYIOVÁ, G.: Škola rozvíjania emocionálnej inteligencie žiakov. 1. vyd. Bratislava: Príroda, 2002, 301 p. ISBN 80-07-01177-3.

GOLEMAN, D.: *Emoční inteligence.* 2. vyd. Praha: Metafora, 1995.

GRESHAM, F. M. – ELLIOTT, S. N.: *Social Skills Rating Systems.* Circle Pines, MN: American Guidance Services, 1990.

GROSSMAN, D. C. – NECKERMAN, H. J. – KOEPSELL, T. D. – LIU, P. Y. – ASHER, K. N. – BELAND, K. – FREY, K. – RIVARA, F. P.: Effectiveness of a violence prevention curriculum among children in elementary school. *Journal of American Medical Association.* 1997, 277 (20), pp. 1605–1611.

GURALNICK, M. J. – NEVILLE, B. – HAMMOND, M. A. – CONNOR, R. T.: The friendships of young children with developmental delays: A longitudinal analysis. *Journal of Applied Developmental Psychology.* 2007, 28, pp. 64–79.

GUZMAN, L. S. – CALL, et al.: Memo: Tauck Family Foundation-Social Competence Item Development and Pilot Project. *Child Trends.* 2014.HOBCRAFT, J. – KIERNAN, K.: Childhood poverty, early motherhood and adult social exclusion. *British Journal of Sociology.* 2001, 52 (3), pp. 495–517.

JORDAN, J. V. – KAPLAN, A. G. – MILLER, J. B. – STIVER, I. P. – SURREY, J. L.: *Women's Growth in Connection: Writings from the Stone Center.* New York, NY: Guilford Press, 1991, 310 p. ISBN978-0898624656.

KOSTER, M. – NAKKEN, H. – PIJL, S. J. – VAN HOUTEN, E. J.: Being part of the peer group: A literature study focussing on the social dimension of inclusion in education. *International Journal of Inclusive Education.* 2009, 13, pp. 117–140.

KROČANOVÁ, Ľ.: Sociálne zručnosti detí so sluchovým postihnutím v bežnej materskej škole. *Efeta.* 2012, 2. roč., XXII, pp. 16–20.

McELWAIN, N. L. – HALBERSTADT, A. G. – VOLLING, B. L.: Mother-reported and father-reported reactions to children's negative emotions: Relations to young children's emotional understanding and friendship quality. *Child Development.* 2007, 78, pp. 1407–1425.

McKEOWN, K. – PRATSCHKE, J. – HAASE, T.: *Family Well-Being: What Makes a Difference?* 2003, 103 p.

MONCHY, M. – PIJL, S. J. – ZANDBERG, T.: Discrepancies in judging social inclusion and bullying of pupils with behaviour problems. *European Journal of Special Needs Education.* 2004, 19 (3), pp. 317–330.

PATRICK, N. J.: *Rozvíjení sociálních dovedností lidí s poruchami autistického spektra: tipy a strategie pro každodenní život.* Praha: Portál, s.r.o., 2011.

ROBERTS, W. – STRAYER, J. Children's anger, emotional expressiveness, and empathy: Relations with parents' empathy, emotional expressiveness, and parenting practices. *Child Development.* 1996, 67, pp. 449–470.

ROGGE, J. U.: Výchova dětí krok za krokem. Praha: Portál, 2007.

ROTHBAUER, M.: *Ako povzbudiť svoje dieťa, aby sa ku mne obracalo s prosbou o radu, alebo pár slov o tom, prečo niektoré deti s rodičmi o svojich problémoch nehovoria.* Nitra: CPPPaP, interný materiál pre rodičov, 2008.

SCHEEPSTRA, A. J. M. – NAKKEN, H. – PIJL, S. J.: Contacts with classmates: The social position of pupils with Down's syndrome in Dutch mainstream education. *European Journal of Special Needs Education*. 1999, 14, pp. 212–220.

SORESI, S. – NOTA, L.: A social skill training for persons with Down's syndrome. *European Psychologist*. 2000, 5 (1), pp. 34–43.

TRLICOVÁ, K.: Sociálny status postihnutého žiaka medzi zdravými. *Psychológia a patopsychológia dieťaťa*. 1995, 30 (3), pp. 302–307.

UČEŇ, I.: Individuálny sociálny status žiakov základných integrovaných škôl verzus postoje k integrácii. *Psychológia a patopsychológia dieťaťa*. 2002, 37 (4), pp. 351–356.

VÁGNEROVÁ, M.: *Psychopatologie pro pomáhající profese*. Praha: Portál, 2008.

ZAHN-WAXLER, C.: The case for empathy: A developmental review. *Psychological Inquiry*. 1991, 2, pp. 155–119.

ZBORTEKOVÁ, K.: Sociálna inklúzia žiakov so sluchovým postihnutím a možnosti jej podpory. *Výchovný aspekt inkluzívnej edukácie a jeho dimenzie*. Bratislava: IRIS, s.r.o., 2012, pp. 260–272.

3 Children with Congenital Sensory Impairment

3.1 Introduction

Considering a relatively broadly conceived title of our project[1], it is necessary to clarify the primary subject of our research within several initial references:

- Since the notion "disability" represents a particularly heterogeneous category including the most varied limitations, it is necessary to define/specify the object of our interest. In our research, we decided to focus our attention on *sensory impairment*. This category can be in fact relatively clearly defined; its degrees are objectively measurable and at the same time, corresponding social impact on quality of life of persons with the given impairment is obvious.

- Within the category of sensory impairment, we decided to examine *hearing and visual* impairment. This is primarily due to the fact that they are so called telereceptors, apparently associated with communication the most and thus, in their very essence, with education and quality of life, too.

- Regarding the perspective of methodology, it is our priority to examine the impact of an existing impairment on quality of life of a child from their earliest age and therefore, we will deal with *congenital impairments or impairments acquired at an early age*. Congenital (or at an early age acquired) visual/hearing impairment is a significant endogenic determinant of a child's further development, quality of their life and their overall prognosis[2].

- Due to the same reason, we will focus on *bilateral visual and hearing impairment*. The ability to perceive auditory/visual stimuli at least by one of the two receptors (i.e. unilateral sensory impairment) enables education to be carried out by more or less standard methods and procedures (there is no need for the Braille alphabet or sign language, etc.). From the perspective of quality of life, it represents a significant difference when compared to bilateral impairments. Even though there are some particularities – e.g. Kral (2012) points out certain vulnerability of children with acquired monocular vision – however, in terms of our re-

1 Quality of Life (of Pupils with Disability) in Cross-modal Perspectives of Inclusive Education.

2 Clearly, social environment of a child, with its unconditionally needed impact, is an absolutely essential and significant exogenous determinant; however, it will not be the subject of the comparative reflection. We would like to discuss specific impacts of the impairment "as such", "an sich", "in itself" on an overall prognosis of child's development.

search topic, bilateral sensory impairments obviously represent a different issue.

- Considering the methodological requirement to select a preferably homogeneous sample of the research population for the analysis and comparison, *we will not deal with combined/ multiple disabilities and distortions* (a combination of sensory impairment with mental or physical disability, autism and other developmental pervasive disorders, etc.). The acceptance of multiple disabilities in selection of the research population would disable drawing generalised conclusions aimed at the phenomenon of sensory impairment as such.

- As regards specific determination of population of children with *sensory impairment, its form and degree* defined by International Classification of Functioning, Disability and Health (ICF), the subject of our research will be a population of children with congenital "severe impairment" to "complete impairment" of "body functions" (ICF, 2001, p. 47) – in our specific case with severe impairment of sensory functions. In case of *sight*, it regards "sensory functions relating to sensing the presence of light and sensing the form, size, shape and colour of the visual stimuli" (ICF, 2001, p. 62). In case of *hearing*, it regards "sensory functions relating to sensing the presence of sounds and discriminating the location, pitch, loudness and quality of sounds" (ICF, 2001, p. 65)[3]. Regarding the topic of our project and the subsequent research, we believe that this approach to classification of sensory impairments is more appropriate than the traditional medical approach determining hearing loss in decibels and loss of sight in percentage[4].

---

3 Due to the possibilities of our research, we will focus predominantly on deaf children communicating in oral language.

4 For the sake of completeness, we provide the following: in terms of visual impairments it regards amblyopia (i.e. limitation of visual functions to 5-15% of normal capacity) and practical blindness or remains of sight with a deficit less than 4% of normal capacity up to maintenance of any ability of visual differentiation – e.g. differentiation of fingers in front of an eye (Vágnerová 2008). Considering hearing impairments, there is a generally acknowledged classification: deafness regards a loss of hearing greater than 110 dB, remains of hearing regard a loss greater than 91 dB and severe hearing loss regards a loss approximately 71-90 dB.

3.2 Possibilities of Creation and Application of Trend Typology in Predicting the Developmental Potential of Children with Disability

Having the population defined in such an operational manner, we would like to focus on the *analysis of its developmental potential and various alternatives of prediction of the developmental trend,* which could be derived on its basis concerning children with sensory impairment (including its immediate limiting impact on quality of their life).

Among several possibilities of application, the analysis of trend functions provides us with suitable foundations and alternatives and covers our needs. In general, based on the *trend typology* and concerning children with sensory impairment, it is possible to distinguish among limited, delayed, interrupted, asymmetric and accelerated type of development[5].

It should not represent labelling in any case; it is a search for a certain platform for possible comparison of consequences of hearing and visual impairment.

- *Limited development* represents an ultimately negative prognosis. It regards severe (mainly organ) impairment that makes it virtually impossible for a child to reach a regular level of development.
- *Delayed development* represents an evident developmental retardation; however, a child has (a hidden or obvious) potential enabling them, under favourable circumstances (e.g. timely intervention, change of environment), to reach a level of regular developmental trend gradually. In case the potential is not used up to a certain age, there is usually a growing risk of limited development including its negative prognosis.
- During the course of regular "normal" ontogenesis, an immediate severe *interruption of development* may occur (for instance, because of loss or damage of hearing, loss or damage of sight) and consequently, there usually occurs *acquired impairment.* After the development was interrupted in this manner, it is possible to predict (depending on specific circumstances) either limited or delayed development (with their above stated characteristics).
- Considering *accelerated development,* an extraordinarily accelerated ("above-normal") course of developmental curve can be observed in

---

5 Certain linearity in characterisation of individual types has a didactic reason here: in fact, it regards extrapolation of various variables that act synergically. However, certain generalisation is necessary for the needs of an input into this analysis.

comparison to the regular standard. Such a developmental trend can be permanent (e.g. above-average gifted children in appropriately stimulating environment) or temporal (e.g. failed perfectionist upbringing or catching up due to a delayed development as a part of a stimulation program).

- *Asymmetric development* is characterised by the fact that some elements of the overall development are delayed; some are in a norm or have also the features of an accelerated development.

This basic trend typology does provide us with an appropriate general insight into developmental classification as a useful basis[6]; however, it does not suffice for our further, more detailed comparison of the development of children with sensory impairments. In fact, it needs to be developed further and specified so that it enables a targeted analysis of individual variables and prediction of further development of a child.

A specific prognosis of development of a particular child with sensory impairment can be derived from this basic trend typology through *systemic examination of individual parts of the specific developmental potential of a child*. We believe that a *model of survey of individual developmental components in the context of a specific sensory impairment* will be the most natural and at the same time the most target-adequate concept for the needs of this application and elaboration of the trend typology. It regards Social, Motor, Emotional, Cognitive and Linguistic component (model acronym: SMECL)[7]. Their order is not supposed to reflect their mutual hierarchical relationship or inner hierarchy: it is obvious that throughout the course of ontogenesis they intersect in a multiple reciprocal feedback.

3.3 A Survey of the Components of Development (Model SMECL) of Children with Sensory Impairments

In accordance with the above-mentioned intentions, we will proceed systematically, according to individual components, which were stated within the basic characterisation of the model SMECL. For the sake of ex-

---

6 Our typology is based on the original typology of developmental disorders by Sovák (1972), which was modified and expanded.

7 Darragh (2010), within her similar model of survey of individual factors determining ontogenesis of a child, speaks of "developmental domains".

actness, we will focus our attention predominantly on children with *congenital blindness and deafness* while mapping the consequences of sensory impairments on the social, motor, emotional, cognitive and linguistic component of development.

It is logical that proportionality of the scope of individual references will vary according to correlation of individual components with the core topic of our research and according to their elaboration in current studies and publications.

Social Component

Prediction of social adaptation, the prognosis of possibilities of social assertion of intact population, is always very delicate and ambiguous: criteria of personal, subjectively assessed success or failure of social adaptation do not have to be identical with generally proclaimed perception (level of education, employment, position in employment, independent living, family, etc.). Regarding persons with disabilities, it applies to subjective perception of social adaptation even more. Considering persons with disabilities, other and completely different and significant variables related to causes, manifestations and consequences of a specific disability and reactions of closer and wider social environment may apply; these variables do not need to be considered in assessment of the social component of SMECL with respect to intact population. Therefore, Požár (2016) aptly states that *any* disability changes social position of a child, who becomes more dependent on the surrounding social environment in majority of cases (which is also being recognised by the society). Moreover, the process of socialisation of children with disability is being complicated by frequent prejudices against persons with disability from the side of majority community (however, on the other hand, children with disability may have several problems with acquisition and interiorisation of social norms related to particularities of their disability). In addition, serious barriers often occur while establishing contacts with the opposite sex, searching for a life partner, establishing a family; inadequate (usually low) self-assessment and a shift in aspiration level may occur, too. The primary disability can thus be secondarily joined by social handicap. The delay in the field of socialisation is thus, in a considerable measure, secondary (Požár 2016).

Considering *deaf children*, Gargiulo (2015) states that the socio-emotional development of children with hearing impairment, recognised in terms of ethnical, age, gender and friends area in the pre-school age, displays the same developmental pattern as in hearing children. However, since the socio-emotional development depends on communicative skills, which are in the case of deaf children modified/reduced depending on the ability of reception and production of sound information, several differences can be observed in the process of socialisation at this age. This includes, for example, the fact that deaf children at this age *prefer pair games to group games* (it may be related to difficulties with attention division, which is predominantly visual in their case, as well as to language difficulties). They also take part in *pretending games* to lesser extent than in thematic, role-playing or model games (possibly due to the negative impact of language deficiencies in the field of understanding and processing imaginary situations) and while playing with deaf peers, they spend significantly less time in cooperative games. Thus, their capacity for receiving and sending language information often limits their socio-emotional growth throughout the development.

It is apparent that one of the dominant roles in social adaptation to the overall community of hearing people is played by the fact whether they use primarily spoken or sign language in their communication with the hearing members of the majority community (being in a relatively better situation in the first case). However, often – mainly with the pre-lingual loss of hearing (and that is the case of our research population) – the process of socialisation of deaf persons is immensely difficult. Their situation is characterised accurately by Vágnerová (2008) as "difficulties in social orientation": since they have difficulties with understanding the current verbal information, norms of behaviour and determination of social roles, worsened social orientation occurs; potentially, they are also less empathetic and they sometimes feel uncertain, even inferior in the communication with the hearing. Therefore, they are at a risk of social isolation in the minority group of persons with hearing impairment (Vágnerová 2008). Similarly, Tarcsiová (2016) claims that problems with acquisition of spoken language cause communication barrier between a deaf individual and the majority society, which is reflected in the psyche of the child, education, possibilities of gaining higher education and thus, social status and a life partner from the majority society. Požár (2016) concludes that the process of socialisation of children with hearing impairment is among the most complicated impairments. They often establish social groups with the character of minorities with a particular culture, communication, etc., which complicates the co-existence with the majority society even more. However, as Gargiulo (2015) points out, modern conveniences such as smartphones, tablets, combined with social media like Facebook and Twitter bring new possibilities of socialisation in the contact with deaf as well as hearing persons – though, a risk as wel.

Vágnerová (2008, p. 200) claims, in regard to socialisation, that *"severe visual impairment* limits the possibility to acquire all the necessary experiences and to learn to react promptly in a required manner".

Among other things, the specific distortion of their non-verbal communication[8] disables an easy and quick orientation in a current social situation, causes a worse level of social understanding, acquisition of social experiences, which often leads to the tendency of social isolation in a familiar environment (Vágnerová 2008, p. 200). In agreement with her, Deiner (2010) states that a child acquires numerous social skills through observation and therefore, a blind child is significantly handicapped in this area. Gargiulo (2015) points out mainly the impossibility to acquire information about a communication partner through visual perception of accompanying signs of communication (e.g. their clothes, the overall appearance, body language), inappropriate ways when eating, etc.; thus, a training of appropriate social behaviour needs to be a part of special stimulation programs. Therefore, it is understandable that lack of contacts with people and lack of social experiences in general can complicate the overall social development of a blind child severely (Požár 2016). Konarska (2010), too, points out frequent isolation and missing contacts with peers as a significant factor of social deprivation. Modern conveniences, however, assist in breaking the social barrier. Šimko and Šimko (2016) draw attention mainly to iPads, iPods, smartphones, and computers with special software for the blind.

Considering the *comparison of blind persons and deaf persons*, it may seem that besides the degree and the form of disability, the level of cognition would be among the most significant factors, dominating from the perspective of success of their social adaptation. However, specific consequences of sensory impairments on the social component of the model SMECL make us consider whether it applies to the observed population, too. Comparing the particularities of social adaptation of persons with visual and hearing impairment, practical experiences and research outcomes certify that blind persons achieve on average a relatively higher level in the field of cognition than deaf persons do. At first sight, it may seem that they should be more successful in social adaptation than deaf persons are. However, deaf persons (in spite of the already mentioned threat of social isolation in a minority group of persons with hearing impairment) have relatively more possibilities in practical life as regards

---

8 In our perception disturbed co-verbal behaviour.

independent employment, social assertion and eventually, the possibility to live an independent life. (For instance, considering the topic of our project, when the possibilities of active participation in spare time activities within inclusive education of blind children and deaf children are compared.) While the beginnings of the development in the social area can be considered in both compared groups in terms of the trend typology to be *delayed*, the perspectives of professional assertion, possibilities of employment, autonomous social adaptation with their consequences on quality of life are usually *limited* to a relatively larger extent for blind persons compared to deaf persons[9]. On the other hand, as Vágnerová (2008) writes, visual impairment belongs to the least socially rejected impairments. However, it is obvious that the level of the social component of the overall development is among the dominant determinants of quality of life of children with sensory visual impairment (the blind) and hearing impairment (the deaf).

Motor Component

The course of acquisition of motor skills is perhaps among the most obvious areas of ontogenesis of a child visible on the outside. Considering the needs of our comparison as well as the aspect of quality of life in general, it is adequate to compare children with visual and hearing impairment separately in terms of the trend of development of gross motor skills and the development of fine motor skills.

Regarding *gross motor skills*, deaf children are usually relatively advantaged here. Let us take into consideration the negative impact of *limited spatial orientation* (closely associated with walking, running, etc.) on the development of gross orientation of *blind persons* in comparison to relatively better possibilities of visual orientation in space of deaf persons (however, deafness has also a specific impact on spatial orientation). According to Kovács (2000), blindness contributes to the development of motor skills negatively since the earliest age. Endogenous pre-programmed spontaneous movements such as lifting arms, legs, grasp reflex to tactile

---

9 Naturally, it does not mean that socialisation of persons with congenital deafness is smooth (see the above stated particularities of the social component of their development) – it is an approximate comparison. If we follow Darragh's (2010) determination of social development as acquisition of the "ability to interact with others in a variety of contexts", we find out that persons with hearing impairment are often significantly limited when it comes to the ability to interact with the hearing persons.

stimuli, etc. do not manifest any variations in the first three months of life. However, movements that are associated with visual stimuli do not appear at this age and thus, the overall development of motor skills of blind children begins to shape differently already at 2-3 months of age in comparison to motor skills of seeing children. Konarska (2010) aptly characterises sight as a "stimulator of motor development", Kochová and Schaeferová (2015) claim the same about the missing motivation (or different motivation compared to seeing persons) for movement. Regarding further development, Vágnerová (2008) states that blind children begin to walk later and their independent locomotion is not spontaneously stimulated as compared to seeing children, quite the contrary. Based on a comparative analysis of research into the development of motor skills of blind children, Walthes (2003) claims that while in statomotor field there are only smaller differences, in locomotion there are considerable differences in comparison to seeing children. However, these differences are not connected to the overall delay of muscular or neuromuscular development of the blind but with the lack of opportunities as well as possibilities of independent locomotion. Moreover, since *the ability of acoustic localisation develops later than the ability of visual localisation*, acoustic signals cannot compensate the missing visual signals at an early age (Walthes 2003). In contrast (see Vágnerová 2008), regarding children with *congenital deafness*, in case of undistorted motor coordination (i.e. undamaged function of statokinetic apparatus – author's note), spatial orientation is usually at a better level from the very beginning than in blind children and it creates a good basis for the overall development of gross motor skills. Krhutová (2011) observes that independent movement and orientation are closely connected to self-service and the freedom of movement is among the essential needs of a man: thus, mobility is a presupposition of independence and breaking away from the dependence on others (Krhutová 2011) and an important attribute of quality of life. From the medical point of view, as Deiner (2010) points out, damage of vestibular apparatus can lead to vertigo with its negative impact on motor coordination.

However, regarding the development of *fine motor skills*, the situation is rather unclear in terms of such a comparison. According to Kábele (in Vágnerová 2008), up to 30 % of children with hearing impairment experience a delayed development of fine motor skills, which can also affect motor skills of articulatory apparatus. However, a change that is connected to the application of compensation methods in education of both kinds of impairment – using Braille alphabet for blind children and sign language and finger spelling alphabet for deaf children, can occur gradually. Their successful training and practical daily application has usually a positive impact on fine motor skills of hands.

After comparing both sensory impairments, it can be stated that the development of gross motor skills is relatively more significantly limited in the case of children with visual impairment. Regarding the area of fine motor skills of articulatory apparatus, the development is more limited in the case of children with hearing impairment. Even though articulation of some speech sounds tends to be divergent in the case of *blind children* and it is usually not that striking for laymen in contrast to the generally recognised typical articulation of deaf children.

Emotional Component

Within the trend typology presented above, the emotional component represents generally a very sensitive and complicated component of development in the case of children with impairment. The manner of realisation of individual coping strategies (i.e. the particularity of coping with the existence of one's impairment[10]) is a permanent process that affects personality of a child with impairment at their most vulnerable places. Daily practice brings various challenges (including the manner and consequence of their solution) for persons with impairment that are associated with the emotional sphere in particular. In case of incorrect, inappropriate coping from the side of the closest surroundings (e.g. tabooing the impairment, neglecting, rejecting a child, etc.), the subsequent negative influence on emotionality and quality of life of the child is inevitable. However, even in case of appropriate coping – appropriate coping with one's impairment, adequate participation in the society, daily life brings situations that a person with impairment often copes with only at the cost of maximal emotional strain. Darragh (2010) states that the development of emotionality does not regard only the ability to control one's emotions effectively, but also the ability to communicate one's emotions.

Considering *blind children, specific limitations* in the field of mimics, which is supposed to accompany emotional movements on the outside[11], as well as social deprivation at an early age in particular, are recognised. It

---

10 Including the simultaneously occurring strategies of closer and wider surroundings coping with the existence of a child with impairment in this surroundings.

11 Thus, an uninformed communication partner may get a false impression of emotional indifference of a blind person.

regards mainly the fear of an unexpected contact with unknown (unseen) objects, persons and events and unexpected sounds (Konarska 2010), but also a relatively frequent problematic mother-child relationship (under-protection and overprotection), which limits the quality of their life in re-spect to the emotional development significantly. The possibly problematic relationship of "reciprocity" mother ↔ blind child is pointed out also by Schmutzler (2006): the fact that a blind child cannot send or receive "nor-mal" nonverbal signals at an early age, can affect a mother stressfully and it can lead to the so-called problematic reciprocity. Garguilo (2015) calls at-tention to a frequently missing smile of blind children as a signal of friend-ly approach and manifestation of empathy, emotions. Požár (2016) stresses that the absence or reduction of expressive movements does not have to be, and obviously is not, an indicator of intensity of inner emotional life of persons with visual impairment. The awareness of limited motor skills, lim-ited mobility and thus, limited independence, which was mentioned above within the motor component of SMECL, can lead to serious frustration of blind persons having the impact on the overall quality of life. Quality of life in this field is also determined by *hearing impairment*. Explosions of anger are often observed at an early age of deaf children, when they can-not express their current need clearly or fail to understand multiply re-peated information coming from a communication partner. Their overall emotional development is often asymmetric, with several lapses mainly in unexpected life situations. Gargiulo (2015) emphasizes that the capacity of deaf children for receiving and sending language information often limits their socio-emotional growth. According to Požár (2016), sometimes they do not understand exactly what other people ask from them; and they are of-ten indifferent to other people's opinion about their behaviour. They have a tendency to react to the obtained information, to the given situation im-pulsively, often irrationally, at the expense of considering effectiveness of such a way of reacting. In the context of the above-mentioned facts and in terms of the applied trend typology, this determination enables us to rea-son that children with hearing impairment as well as children with visual impairment apparently display *asymmetric development* of emotionality.

Linguistic Component

Within our comparison, the linguistic component can be divided– simi-larly to the motor component – into two areas. In this case, it will regard the area of content (acquisition of symbolic processes, known in English under the term "language") and the external, formal area (acquisition of non-symbolic processes, i.e. phonetic aspect – pronunciation, expressed in English by the term "speech"). Obviously, considering quality of life, the acquisition of symbolic processes is far more important; however, the external phonetic aspect of language is significant.

A relatively more serious situation than that of blind children can be usually observed in *deaf children*. The success of their education is often *limited* mainly by the problematic way of acquisition of abstract notions and in oral language communication it is limited also by perceiving and articulating phonemes and clusters, which cannot be well lip-read or require a more demanding articulation (for example, consonant clusters, velars, alveolars). However, cochlear implants for children with hearing impairment have brought a revolutionary breakthrough in this developmental component (including the subsequent impact on the improvement of quality of life). It can be justifiably expected that due to their further improvement and wide-spread usage, a shift from the category "deaf" to the category "hard of hearing" will occur in case of many children with such an impairment. Considering the way of their communication, Požár (2016) states that preferring the sign language leads to their exclusion or does not contribute to their inclusion into the majority society, respectively. A solution may be the preference for *bilingual education*, while sign language can be understood as a certain stepping stone to managing the language of the majority, i.e. the common spoken language. If Darragh (2010) distinguishes between "social English" (social Slovak in our environment) related to common, everyday spoken and written communication and "academic English" (academic Slovak, here) necessary for success in school education, it should be claimed that in our environment it is "social Slovak" and not "academic Slovak" that is typical of persons with congenital deafness.

The linguistic component has its particularities in the case of *blind children*, too. Our research studies (Lechta 1988) and relevant authors (Sovák 1981; Fromm-Degenhardt 1990; Šimko-Šimko 2010) point out a delay in their speech development (that is usually gradually corrected at school age mainly due to the compensation effect of acquisition of Braille alphabet). The delay is caused predominantly by reduced possibilities of experimentation and imitation at an early age (Lechta 2011). However, *verbalism of blind persons* is among those particularities that remain. Even though, children with congenital blindness gradually learn to use several terms based on visual experience (e.g. terms related to colours) in a correct communication context. However, because of the missing sensory experience, the *asymmetry in the development of communicative competence* manifests itself in the fact that these terms do not have a corresponding sensory basis and they are so-called "empty concepts". Thus, verbalism is a typical impact of congenital blindness; Konarska (2010) characterises it accurately as a result of "hypercompensation". Moreover, characteristic particularities in the development of the pragmatic level of language of children with congenital blindness need to be mentioned, too; they originate as a result of the missing visual contact and the possibilities of imitation of speech/communication pattern through the visual way. Usually it regards *disturbed coverbal behaviour*, i.e. behaviour in the course of the act of communication, interfering with the intention of communication of a blind child (Lechta 1989), e.g. dull facial expression ("poker face") suggesting, as mentioned above, a false impression of their indifference; swaying from side to side while speaking; supplying visual contact with tactile contact (touching communication partner while speaking), etc. Sometimes visually inadequate articulation (e.g. incorrect, interdental pronunciation of various phonemes) caused by the impossibility to imitate the manner of articulation of the closest surroundings by the visual way can be discovered. Based on the outcomes of research and observations of communication of these children, Požár (2016) concludes: they show a lowered voice variation, they lack appropriate voice modulation. In contrast to the regularly seeing they have a tendency to talk more loudly, more slowly, with typical irrational gestures and unsuitable pantomimics, they do not move lips as intensively as the intact while articulating. It is obvious that severe congenital sensory impairments tend to limit the overall area of linguistic development; therefore, *following the applied trend typology, not only delayed development but in case of severe impairment also limited development may occur and in cases of disproportional acquisition of "language" and "speech" asymmetric development may occur.* In cases of pre-lingual loss of hearing or sight of a child after their birth (i.e. before acquisition of mother tongue), considering the linguistic component, *interrupted* and later delayed or limited development will often occur.

Cognitive Component

Cognitive processes represent an "output" of an organism on a man's journey through life, determining quality of their life significantly. Considering congenital sensory impairments, these processes are limited by several ways. As Kral (2012) claims, many cognitive functions are immediately associated with sensory system; thus, missing hearing or sight are inevitably reflected in the field of cognition immediately. Besides, dialectic interconnectedness of linguistic and cognitive development naturally results into the fact that limitations in the field of language acquisition are manifested in the context of its feedback relationship with the cognitive area also in cognitive processes (and vice versa). It relates mainly to symbolic processes (following the above-characterised "language") whose *limited development* is immediately reflected into the linguistic field as well as the cognitive component.

Concerning *blind children,* clearly, a delayed development of cognitive processes applies at an early age: an apparent retardation impact of missing visual perceptions on the cognitive development is prominent. Besides, Konarska (2010) points out that the lack of visual stimulation can be manifested negatively in a sort of "motor apathy", which can be displayed gradually as lowered "emotional-motivational tension" with a negative impact on the development of their cognitive activities. Kovács (2000) highlights the negative consequence of missing association "sound↔seeing the object that is the source of the sound" on the cognitive development as well as the negative impact of fear of mobility and motor passivity on the quantity and quality of obtained information about the surrounding environment and cognition as such. A summarising and apt conclusion was provided by Illyés (1968, p.88), "a distinctive blind person's relationship between the concrete sensory cognition and abstract mental cognition". Lányi (1968) adds that a blind person depends more on abstraction in the process of cognition; language, the privileged tool of intellect, has a tremendous importance in the development of cognitive functions. However, the prognosis of further development is relatively positive: the already mentioned compensation influence of communication (obtaining of information) by Braille alphabet in an appropriately stimulating environment has a positive impact on the cognitive component, too. In spite of the fact, that congenital visual impairment influences the development of cognitive processes (while the compensation function is, naturally, represented predominantly by aural perception and tactile perception), Vágnerová (2008) stresses that the overall level of verbal intelligence is not directly dependent on visual impairment. If such an individual has at least average preconditions and lives in a stimulating environment, the delayed development of their intelligence does not occur. However, Kochová and Schaeferová (2015) emphasise that in regard to blind children, the mechanism of creation of ideas and the subsequent thought processes may due to the lack of visual perceptions take place on the basis of different (for a given object not always essential) dominant features as compared to the seeing children.

A worse developmental prognosis is usually noted for *deaf children*. Limitations in the field of symbolic processes are often manifested in their overall cognitive development in a retarding manner. The missing hearing may be displayed negatively in the field of understanding causality, understanding cause-consequence events and in anticipatory behaviour. This fact has been confirmed by results of several studies. At present, based on a summary of studies on cognitive functions of deaf children, Kral (2012) states that deafness results into a reduced capacity of short-term memory. In his opinion, deafness affects the early development of motor skills negatively as well (probably because motor skills and hearing interact with each other throughout the process of neuronal activity) with further negative impacts on cognition. In addition, attention of deaf children is oriented more on the visual periphery, which impacts the development of the ability of long-term maintenance of attention on a specific object (sustained attention) negatively, with a negative impact on acquisition of skills that a child acquires by observing their parents. Požár (2016) asserts that children with a severe hearing impairment have often problems with understanding information they were given and with understanding norms of behaviour. A possible limiting impact of reduced cognitive level of some persons with hearing impairment is pointed out by Potměšil (2011), too: the inability to apply information and knowledge in planning and implementing the decision-making process is reflected negatively also in self-reflection of a deaf person. However, based on studies on the relationship between IQ and the level of hearing impairment, Lányi (1968) points out that even a severe hearing impairment does not exclude a priori exceptional intelligence.

3.4 Conclusion

To sum up, it may be stated that children with sensory impairment manifest several specific features of development in the monitored components of our SMECL model. Following a comparison and summary of several studies in the field of the development of deaf children, Plutecka (2013) claims, that they demonstrate specific features in the field of motor skills as well as emotional and social development. Despite being exposed to the same cognitive stimuli as hearing children, they operate with a different cognitive substrate and different intellectual processes than hearing children. Equally, based on the Lewis and Maurer concept of sensitive phases of child's development, Kral (2012) states that in regard to children with congenital blindness and deafness several essential developmental steps are squandered due to the lack of sensory stimuli and these steps cannot be caught up with even despite the plasticity of a child's nervous system[12]. Nevertheless, Walthes (2003) claims that particularities of the motor, linguistic, socio-emotional and cognitive development of blind children do not represent an unsolvable problem if stimulated in an appropriate environment.

World Health Organisation characterises quality of life as a phenomenon that is related to an *individual's perception of their position in life in the context of culture and value systems they live in and in relationship to their goals, expectations, norms and fears.* If the focus of this definition is examined, following the above-mentioned particularities of SMECL model, it can be stated that perception of one's position, relationship to one's goals, expectations, norms and fears has its considerable particularities in regard to children with congenital deafness and blindness. The context of culture and value systems they live in display these particularities, too (cf. community of intact children versus a child with impairment, community of parents of intact children versus parents of a child with impairment, etc.). However, there exist specific differences among the individual types of sensory impairments in the given correlations. For example, one of the first studies in this field in our region (Dolejš 2015) proved that among the pupils with visual impairment those pupils who attended special schools reached higher quality of life than their peers educated in an integrated way. On the contrary, among the pupils with hearing impairment the pupils educated in integrated conditions reached higher quality of life than the pupils educated in special schools.

In order to enable successful implementation of the idea of inclusion to educational practice, it is necessary to search for means of dynamic stabilisation of social culture: on the one hand, by providing social roles accen-

---

12 According to the conception of sensitive phases, promoted already by M. Montessori, mental development of a man does not take place at random; it is determined by transitionally incoming phases of increased sensitivity in respect to acquisition of the most varied abilities and skills. This escalated sensitivity, focused on a specific direction, dies down after some time (like a light beam illuminating only some objects, while others remain in the dark; afterwards, the beam moves on). A child needs different stimuli in respect to their actual sensitive phase at each stage of its development. When the sensitive period passes away, acquisition of certain qualities and skills requires a much greater effort.

tuating responsibility; on the other hand, by enabling mutual contact and meetings accentuating social attractiveness (Gajdošíková Zeleiová 2011). This confirms the legitimacy of the thesis postulated by the researchers of the submitted project that congenital sensory impairment (congenital blindness and deafness) displays such significant features in regard to quality of life that its comprehensive examination in multiple perspectives of inclusive education is meaningful and its outcomes can contribute to the development of the given field.

Literature

DARRAGH, J.C.: *Introduction to Early Childhood Education.* Equity and Inclusion. Boston: Pearson 2010. ISBN 978-0-205-56954-0.

DEINER, P.L.: *Inclusive Early Childhood Education.* Wadsworth: Cengage Learning: 2010. ISBN 978-1-4283-2086-4.

DOLEJŠ, V.: *Kvalita života žiakov s postihnutím v základných školách.* Dizertačná práca. Trnava: PdFTU2015.

FARKAS, M. – PERLUSZ, A.: A hallássérült gyermekek óvodai és iskolai nevelése és oktatása. In ILLYÉS, S. (ed.). *Gyógypedagógiai alapismeretek.* Budapest: ELTE 2000, ISBN 9-63-715528-7, pp .505 – 534.

FROMM, W. – DEGENHARDT, R. a kol.: *Rehabilitationspädagogik für Sehgeschädigte.* Berlin: Volk und Gesundheit 1990. ISBN 3-333-00386-4.

GAJDOŠÍKOVÁ ZELEIOVÁ, J.: Psychosociálne faktory tvorby inkluzívneho sociálneho prostredia v triede. In LECHTA, V. (ed.). *Inkluzívna edukácia ako multidimenzionálny výchovný problém.* Inklusive Edukation als mehrdimensionales Erziehungsproblem. Bratislava: IRIS 2011, pp. 76 – 84.

GARGIULO, R.M.: *Special Education in Contemporary Society.* Los Angeles: SAGE 2015. ISBN 978-1-4522-1677-5.

ILLYÉS, S.: A látási fogyatékosok (vakok) gondolkodása, beszéde. In ILLYÉS, G. – ILLYÉS, S. – JANKOVICH, L. – LÁNYI, M.: *Gyógypedagógiai pszichológia.* Budapest: Akadémiai kiadó 1968, pp. 96 – 68.

INTERNATIONAL CLASSIFICATION OF FUNCTIONING, DISABILITY AND HEALTH. Geneva: WHO 2001. ISBN 92 4 154542 9.

KOCHOVÁ, K. – SCHAEFEROVÁ, M.: *Dítě s postižením zraku.* Praha: Portál 2015. ISBN 978-80-262-0782-5.

KONARSKA, J.: *Rozwój i wychowanie rehabilitujace dziecka niewidzacego w okresie wczesnego i średnieho dzieciństwa.* Kraków: Wydawnictwo Naukowe Uniwesytetu Pedagogiczneho 2010. ISBN 978-83-7271-887-6.

KOVÁCS, K.: Látássérült gyermekek az óvodában és az iskolában. In ILLYÉS, S. (ed.).

Gyógypedagógiai alapismeretek. Budapest: ELTE 2000, ISBN 9-63-715528-7, pp. 461 – 504.

KRAL, A.: Frühe Hörerfahrung und sensible Phasen. In LEONHARDT, A. (ed.). *Frühes Hören*. Hörschädigungen ab dem ersten Lebenstag erkennen und therapieren. München-Basel: Ernst Reinhardt Verlag 2012, ISBN 978-3-497-02288-5, pp. 26 – 46.

KRHUTOVÁ, L.: Lidé se zrakovým postižením a pomáhajíci profese. In MICHALÍK, J. a kol.: *Zdravotní postižení a pomáhající profese*. Praha: Portál, 2011. ISBN 978-80-7367-859-3, pp. 269 – 346.

LÁNYI, M.: A látási fogytékosok inteligenciája. A hallási fogyatékosok inteligenciája. In ILLYÉS, G. – ILLYÉS, S. – JANKOVICH, L. – LÁNYI, M.: *Gyógypedagógiai pszichológia*. Budapest: Akadémiai kiadó 1968, pp. 96 – 98; 137 – 140.

LECHTA, V.: *Možnosti rozvíjania reči u nevidiacich detí*. Paedagogica specialis XIV-XV, Bratislava: SPN 1988, pp. 75 – 82.

LECHTA, V.: *Gestörtes koverbales Verhalten in der logopädischen Praxis*. Wissenschaftliche Zeitschrift der Humboldt-Univerzität zu Berlin 38, 989, č.7, pp. 806 – 807.

LECHTA, V.: *Symptomatické poruchy řeči u dětí*. Praha: Portál 2011. ISBN 978-80-7367-977-4.

PLUTECKA, K.: *Ojciec wobec osiagnieć edukacyjnych dziecka nieslyszacego*. Kraków : Wydawnictwo Naukove Uniwersytetu Pedagogicznego 2013. ISBN 978-83-7271-795-5.

POTMĚŠIL, M.: Osoby se sluchovým postižením jako cílová skupina. In MICHALÍK, J. a kol.: *Zdravotní postižení a pomáhající profese*. Praha: Portál 2011. ISBN 978-80-7367-859-3, pp. 347 – 408.

POŽÁR, L.: Psychologické determinanty inkluzivní pedagogiky. In LECHTA, V.: *Inkluzivní pedagogika*. Praha: Portál 2016, pp. 96-110. ISBN 978-80-262-1123-5.

POŽÁR, L.: *Základy psychológie ľudí s postihnutím*. Trnava: TU 2007. ISBN 978-80-8082-147-0.

SCHMUTZLER, H. – J.: *Handbuch Heilpädagogisches Grundwissen*. Freiburg-Basel-Wien: Herder 2006. ISBN 978-3-451-29197-5.

SOVÁK, M.: *Nárys speciální pedagogiky*. Praha: SPN 1972.

SOVÁK, M.: *Uvedení do logopedie*. Praha: SPN 1981. ISBN 14-530-78.

ŠIMKO, J. – ŠIMKO, M.: Zrakové postižení. In LECHTA, V. (ed.). *Základy inkluzivní pedagogiky*. Praha: Portál 2010. ISBN 978-80-7367-679-7, pp. 200 – 215.

TARCSIOVÁ, D.: *Sluchové postižení jako pedagogický fenomén*. In LECHTA, V. (ed.). Inkluzivní pedagogika. Praha: Portál 2016, pp. 257-262. ISBN 978-80-262-1123-5.

VÁGNEROVÁ, M. *Psychopatologie pro pomáhajíci profese*. Rozšířené a přepracované vydání. Praha: Portál 2008. ISBN 978-80-7367-414-4.

WALTHES, R.: Symptomatik, Ätologie und Diagnostik bei Beeinträchtigung der visuellen Wahrnehmung. In LEONHARDT, A. – WEMBER, F. B.: *Grundfragen der Sonderpädagogik*. Weinheim, Basel, Berlin: Beltz Verlag 2003, ISBN 3-407-57204-2, pp. 349 – 375.

WHOQOL GROUP: World Health Organisation Quality of Life Assessment. In *World Health Forum*, 1996, Vol. 17, № 4, pp. 354 – 356.

4 Quality of Life of Pupils with Sensory Impairment in Non-formal Education

4.1 Introduction

Leisure time as a space of non-formal education is usually considered one of the areas of assessment of quality of life of an individual. Subjective satisfaction with utilisation of leisure time, its capacity and available possibilities of actualisation are commonly included within the indicators of quality of life. However, the area of leisure time and thus, non-formal education, too, which represents a natural part of out-of-school life among children and the youth, is not included in all concepts of quality of life. The WHO places leisure time activities in a thematically heterogeneous area environment (WHOQOL-100), which through its focus significantly exceeds other areas (physical health, mental health, degree of independence, social relations, and spiritual area). An individual area leisure time is contained, for example, in the Canadian and Washington Concept of Quality of Life (Baran, Baraniewicz 2016), the concept of Graham et al. (1997), in which leisure time activities are indicated at the second place. Recreation and leisure time activities have formed a constant area in the measurement tools of quality of life since the 1980s and according to Doležalová, Ondráková and Nowosad (2011), they represent one of the nine factors based on which an individual subjectively assesses the quality of his/her life. Leisure time occurs more frequently in the tools aimed at adult population rather than at children and the youth. This area is absent in the most frequented tools of quality of life related to health; the questions regarding spending of leisure time are mostly represented in another area, most frequently in the area of social relations or social life, for instance, Quality of Life Questionnaire, KINDL, KIDCSREEN. The absence of leisure time as an individual area in standardised tools can be considered a certain paradox, since leisure time activities undoubtedly contribute to quality of life of an individual. It has been confirmed by a number of renowned specialists (e.g. Aitchison 2003; Kassing et al. 2010; Anderson 2012) and providers of leisure time activities themselves. For example, in the Position Statement on Inclusion of National Recreation and Park Association in the USA, it is stated that "through leisure an individual gains an enhanced sense of competence and self-direction; a healthy leisure lifestyle can prevent illness and promote wellness; the social connection with one's peers plays a major role in his/her life satisfaction; the opportunity to choose is an important component in one's quality of life" (NRPA 1999). Aitchison (2003) argues in favour of the benefit of leisure time activities in a similar manner: "increasing self-esteem, confidence and psychological well-being; enhancing physical health and fitness; reducing the risk of illness; contributing towards positive social interaction and relationships". Recreation as a synonym of leisure time has also a therapeutic significance for individuals with disability. A scientific field – therapeutic recreation – originated in the USA in the past century; a professional organisation uniting experts The American Therapeutic Recreation Association was established (1986) and a professional journal Therapeutic Recreation Journal has been issued regularly since 1966. Therapeutic recreation that uses leisure time activities intentionally to improve health, functional possibilities, independence and quality of life (NTRS 2000) represents a research contribution in the following areas: physical health and its support; cognitive functionality; psychosocial health; growth, personal and life satisfaction (Shank et al. 1993). It is obvious that leisure time activities, and at the same time non-formal education, contribute to quality of life of an individual; the question is whether they lead to improvement of overall quality of life or its partial areas, for example, sporting activities and the physical area, artistic activities and the emotional area, etc.

Activities taking place within non-formal education have a broad scope, and their contribution for an individual cannot be clearly determined or defined. It follows from the merit of functions of non-formal education, which are usually narrowed into the level of formation, recreation, socialisation, self-actualisation and prevention (Kratochvílová 2010), while the quantification of functions of leisure time as a space for non-formal education is significantly broader. According to the findings of a British study, participation of pupils with disability in leisure time activities in an inclusive environment contributes to the following: improving the physical wellbeing; experiencing psychological sense of belonging; experiencing satisfaction in acquiring social experiences; experiencing a success; developing skills and learning; and participation in social life (Baran, Baraniewicz 2016). Similar findings emerged from the research of Eriksson and Granlund (2004). According to them, children and adolescents with disability perceive participation as an opportunity to: strengthen self-respect, self-esteem; establish friendships: affiliation to a group, experiencing interaction with other people; carry out activities: development of interests, active activity, not only presence; self-determination: to have an opportunity to influence a situation, to have an opportunity and be capable of a choice, to make decisions and to organise.

Functions of non-formal education and key areas of quality of life contained in the standardised tools are intertwined: self-actualisation is projected into emotional well-being and self-competence, socialisation into social and emotional well-being, recreation (also referred to as health-hygienic function) into physical well-being. Due to the complexity of non-formal education, it is relatively difficult to empirically grasp and describe its contribution so that it could be clearly and methodologically correctly detected in relation to quality of life, which is, after all, reflected in hetero-geneity of methodological approaches and designs of the research in question. Researchers generally focus on a selected aspect of non-formal educa-tion, that they link with perceived, or attributed quality of life, for example, they examine correlations between participation in leisure time activities and perceived quality of life; they explore the impact of a specific leisure time activity on quality of life based on input and output measurements; they research perceived value of non-formal education and propose its significance for quality of life; they observe outcomes of non-formal edu-cation and assess their contribution to quality of life; they point out to the barriers of non-formal education and their impact on quality of life of an individual, etc. The last-mentioned aspect in particular is relatively often a subject to research, since inclusive conditions are created rather slowly in an ordinary environment, even in spite of the fact that the ideas of inclu-sion are being gradually legislatively rooted in individual countries, mainly due to the ratification of the UN Convention on the Rights of Persons with Disabilities. The importance of non-formal education is pointed out by the European Agency for Special Needs and Inclusive Education in a material entitled Key Principles for Promoting Quality of Inclusive Education – Re-commendations for Policy Makers (2011), which requires that pupils with specific needs participate in extracurricular and leisure time activities ac-tively. Young people themselves stated at the past hearing in the European Parliament (2015) that they feel strong support from youth organisations – a component of non-formal education, which, according to them, should be systematically involved in the decision-making processes about young people with specific needs.

4.2 Research on Quality of Life in Non-formal Education

Research that examines connections between non-formal education and quality of life related to health has several limits in the context of the thematic framework of the monograph – inclusive education of pupils with sensory impairment. The first limit is that most standardised tools through which the participation in non-formal education is explored, mainly the Children's Assessment of Participation and Enjoyment (King et al. 2004), do not primarily differentiate the environment of implementation of activities into segregated and inclusive. These tools mostly examine the measure of the environment organisation, i.e. whether a participant carries out more activities within his/her family, in the company of parents, siblings, or in a broader social, mostly organised, environment. Even though the tool offers a relatively detailed picture of a respondent's participation in formal and non-formal activities according to intensity, diversity and type of their focus (recreational, physical, social, skill-based, and self-improvement), it does not provide possibilities of an exact differentiation of the environment. On the other hand, in certain cases it is illogical to distinguish the type of educational environment, since some individuals carry out the activities both in segregated and inclusive environment. A research conducted by the National Children and Youth Institute in the Czech Republic (2010) demonstrated a demand from the side of parents so that children with disability would carry out activities also in homogeneous groups, since they need models that would show them how to live fully with a disability; they need to have a contact with "their kind" and specialised activities moderate the impacts of disability, e.g. training of spatial orientation for the blind, acquisition of abstract notions for the deaf, etc. According to Clarke (2006), the choice of inclusive or segregated environment represents a certain tension for parents, because some of them see the best opportunities for their child precisely within the intact peers, the others, particularly parents of children with severe and multiple disabilities, prefer segregated environment due to individual support and professional approach. In a research by Keil et al. (2001), 11 % of inquired parents expressed themselves in favour of specialised activities for pupils with visual impairment up to the age of 16. Some parents prefer segregated activities due to negative experiences from ordinary environment; for example, Tsai, Fung (2009) state that parents of children with intellectual disability resigned on inclusive activities after being rejected by personnel or intact participants and as the main reasons they state negative attitudes and lack of understanding of persons with intellectual disability. The visually impaired state, beside the negative attitudes, also inappropriate reactions to blindness or an unusual eye movement or problems in social skills (Gold et al. 2010). At the same time, the specialised conditions are positively assessed by the participants with disability themselves, since there do not occur barriers present in the ordinary environment and friendships with equally impaired peers are supported – an important source of emotional support in sharing the same experiences (cf. Beresford, Clarke 2009). Some studies from the past have even pointed out negative relationship between participation in inclusive conditions and quality of life. For example, in regard to pupils with learning disability it was discovered that team sport activities requiring quick reaction abilities can lead to lowered self-respect or give a feeling of failure; considering pupils with physical disability they can arouse a feeling of insufficiency, lowered self-esteem and self-respect (Beresford, Clarke 2009). On the contrary, other researches indicate that pupils with impairment are happier and display higher quality of life if they are in an inclusive environment (Schleien, Green, Stone 2003). In addition, in an experiment conducted by Hutzler, Chacham-Guber, Reiter (2013), it was confirmed that pupils display better quality of life and perceived social competence if they attend a reverse-integrated basketball activity rather than a competitive or recreational activity in a segregated environment. Therefore, some studies examine the connection between non-formal education and quality of life without regard to the nature of the environment, even if they differentially state the numbers of pupils from special and regular schools while presenting the research sample (e.g. Kelly et al. 2012, Shihako-Thomas et al. 2012).

Researches in which one of the tools of health-related quality of life and Children's Assessment of Participation and Enjoyment – CAPE (King et al. 2004) was used provide a relatively complex and exact image of correlations between non-formal education and quality of life within available research design. Since the tools are standardised and the relations between the researched phenomena are expressed at the level of correlations, the findings from individual researches can be mutually compared. At the same time, the structure of the CAPE tool enables the researchers to gain a greater spectrum of data than in researches in which participation is assessed according to a single aspect, mostly frequency, length of duration or content. Surprisingly, available findings from these researches are not consistent. For example, Shikako-Thomas et al. (2012) found out in pupils with cerebral palsy that the intensity of participation significantly correlates with physical and psychosocial well-being. From the perspective of the typology of activities – recreational, physical, social, self-improvement and skill-based, in regard to the skill-based activities, no influence on physical well-being was discovered in connection to intensity or diversity. Comparable findings resulted from a similar research on pupils with spinal cord injury (Kelly et a. 2012), according to which, participation in organised activities contributes to higher quality of life in social and school area and in overall; participation in heterogeneous groups contributes to higher quality of life in emotional area, intensity of participation in physical and social activities correlates with quality of life. On the contrary, different findings resulted from an analogical research on pupils with muscular dystrophy (Bendixen et al. 2012). Authors did not discover a connection between participation in leisure time activities and quality of life; differences were not demonstrated in the control intact group either. However, the research confirmed current findings in the fact that pupils with physical disability carry out less physical activities and have lower quality of life, mainly in the physical area, than their intact peers (statistically significant differences were demonstrated in all areas except for the emotional area).

Ambiguous findings can be found also in researches on intact pupils, for example, the Turkish authors Gülşah, Can, Gözaydin (2011) discovered that implementation of leisure time activities had different impact on quality of life of boys and girls. A regular physical activity in duration of one year contributed to higher quality of life in the area of physical well-being and social functionality in regard to boys; however, in regard to girls, no changes were displayed. In addition, according to the findings by Lacy et al. (2011), boys who carried out a regular physical activity displayed higher quality of life than girls who participated in these activities under the same conditions. Despite the sporadic occurrence of opposing findings, majority of researches confirm a positive connection between non-formal education and quality of life in regard to pupils with disability and without disability. A significant relationship between these phenomena is demonstrated mainly by researches of experimental or quasi-experimental character. Educational programs that are validated in such researches have often a higher intensity and a more elaborated content and thus, the resulting significance is higher than common programs. An example might be a study by Eratay (2013), according to which, participation in an intensive half a yearlong program of non-formal education contributed to improvement of self-control, coping with aggression and cognitive skills in pupils with intellectual disability.

Another limit is represented by the fact that many researches are focused on connections between non-formal education and a selected aspect of quality of life, for instance, a physical, mental or social aspect and they do not reflect the overall image of quality of life as a multidimensional construct. Even though these researches confirm a positive correlation, they do not address all areas in which quality of life of an individual is improved. For example, an analytical study of the Canadian authors Dahan-Oliel, Shikako-Thomas, Majnemer (2012) summarising 19 researches on participation in leisure time activities of pupils with neurodevelopmental disabilities results into the following connections: 1) participation in leisure time activities is positively reflected in physical well-being, 2) participation in leisure time activities of diverse orientation has a positive impact on the development of intrapersonal aspects of a personality (e.g. self-respect, self-perception, self-confidence, etc.), 3) participation in leisure time activities is positively reflected in emotional and social well-being, 4) participation in leisure time activities supports cognition, 5) leisure time interests and their implementation support subjective well-being. The authors recorded also negative aspects of participation that were connected to inadequate adaptation of conditions, barriers and limits. According to Beresford and Clarke (2009), participation in non-formal education positively influences physical and psychological well-being, belonging, enjoyment, social outcomes, experiences of success, skills and learning, community based experiences. It is also clear that pupils who participate in leisure time activities have more friends than those who do not take part in them (Beresford, Clarke, 2009). McConkey et al. (2012), who evaluated the contribution of an international project Unified Sport attended by participants with mental disability (92 % attended a special school), their intact peers and coaches from five European countries (Germany, Hungary, Poland, Serbia, Ukraine), clarified the contribution of the project in the context of four key topics: a) personal development, b) inclusive and friendly bonds, c) positive perception of persons with mental disability, d) establishment of a local community. A qualitative analysis of an interview with 40 respondents from each country revealed that participation in the project and its media coverage contributed to improvement of the social status of participants with disability at school and in the community. It led to improvement of interpersonal and intrapersonal competencies, communicative skills, self-confidence and self-respect; it also influenced the intact peers and their parents to promote the idea of inclusion, to cooperate further and to support inclusion at the local level (McConkey et al. 2012, p. 8).

Other researches enable to identify the influence of non-formal education on quality of life indirectly. For example, Bizová (2016) found out that pupils with specific needs displayed various types of social interactions in inclusive environment depending on the character of non-formal education. Accepting social interactions occurred more frequently in structured and guided activities than in recreational ones, into which a pedagogue did not interfere. Other researches indicate an impact of non-formal activities on the social component of quality of life. For instance, Hewett et al. (2012) discovered that 76 % of pupils with sensory impairment aged 14 – 17 have a daily Internet access and use social networks predominantly. 91 % out of these pupils have a social network profile and 25 % use it for contact with friends. 75 % of the respondents have a smartphone and 93 % of the respondents use it for contact with friends and family. Similar findings emerged from the research of Gold et al. (2010) according to which, three quarters of the respondents with sensory impairment socialise online and 26 % confirmed that they had known new people through the electronic access. Social support plays an important role in prevention of socio-pathological phenomena (Dědová, 2015, 2016). In spite of the fact that these researches do not clarify all connections between non-formal education and quality of life, they can be considered a relevant source in proving a positive impact of leisure time activity on quality of life of an individual.

The third limit resides in the fact that in some researches with a heterogeneous research sample, individual types of disabilities are not differentiated in the analysis of findings and interpretations of findings, but the findings are presented in overall, representing the research group as such without mentioning any partial differences. Such an approach is usually chosen by researchers intentionally in order to detect common and not different elements. Consequently, it is not possible to find out whether there are any differences among pupils with sensory impairment and other impairments from the perspective of the research subject, since the character of impairments would indicate them. This approach can be discovered in past and current researches, too; for example, Shields and Synnot (2016) examined barriers of participation in sport activities in pupils with cerebral palsy, visual impairment and intellectual disability. They pointed out to shared barriers: lack of professional skills and willingness of personnel to fulfil the ideas of inclusion, negative attitudes toward the participants with disability and lack of opportunities in the inclusive environment. In regard to pupils with sensory impairment, architectonic barriers (orientation in the facility and during implementation of an activity) may come to the front; in pupils with cerebral palsy – procedural barriers (adjustment of conditions of an activity implementation depending on the level of disability); and in pupils with learning disability it may be attitude barriers (acceptance of lowered reaction ability, lower mental level in comparison to intact pupils of the same age). For instance, in the research of Nzegwu, Dooley (2008), pupils with visual impairment stated sight and physical condition as the main reason of non-participation in leisure time activities; further, it was the lack of information, financial means, opportunities, technical side of an activity and concern of their parents about safety. On the contrary, the research conducted by Stuart, Liebermanm, Hand (2006) brought findings consistent with the research of Shields, Synnot (2016).

Blind pupils aged 10-12 perceived the following as a barrier of participation in sport activities: others laughing at them, lack of opportunities and possibilities of participation with the intact participants. Partially sighted pupils pointed out to uncertainty in what is required from them and in accordance with the blind pupils they pointed out to the lack of opportunities of participation and mockery from the side of the intact participants. Parents' attitudes differed only in the fact that in regard to the blind pupils they were concerned the most about accidents and in regard to the partially sighted pupils they pointed out to the insufficiently trained personnel. Even if the common findings are of importance and have their justification, in terms of an intentional application of findings into practice, researches with differentiated approach have some benefits. For example, while comparing the limits of participation and habitual physical activity in more than 900 pupils with hearing, visual, physical impairment and chronic medical disability, Longmuier and Bar-Or (2000) found out that pupils with visual impairment have the least physical activity and the most limits of participation in sport activities than other pupils do. On the contrary, pupils with hearing impairment displayed the best results in all surveyed areas, and a sedentary type of activity was demonstrated more frequently by older than younger pupils within the overall research group. Decrease in physical activity in pupils with visual impairment at older age was confirmed also by a research of Ayvazoglu, Hyun-Kyoung, Kozub (2006) that, among other things, showed that pupils carry out more physical activities if their siblings and parents do so.

4.3 Conclusion

Based on the above-mentioned facts it is possible to describe the research in connections between non-formal inclusive education and quality of life as closely profiled. In spite of the fact that the issue of quality of life related to health has been a subject of an intense interest of specialists in the past two decades, a relatively low number of researches covering the field of our interest is to be found in scientific journals and databases of scientific studies. Generally, it can be stated that research on quality of life is focused on connections with determining factors, such as the rate of anxiety, stress, victimisation, social support, health condition, school success, etc. rather than the connections with non-formal education in inclusive environment. The combination of non-formal education, quality of life and a determining factor occurs more frequently in researches on adult population not concerning the environment of activities implementation. For example, Vanner et al. (2008) discovered that a higher level of physical and leisure time activity in adults associates with a lower level of apathy and depression and a higher level of cognition, efficiency, physical and mental quality of life. Researchers from Spain and the USA (Garcia-Villamisar, Dattilo 2010) similarly discovered positive changes in the score of stress, satisfaction and productivity in participants with autism spectrum disorder; however, irrelevant changes in the area of independence and social domain after a yearlong participation in an intensive leisure time program in segregated environment. Likewise, Motl et al. (2013) discovered in respondents with multiple sclerosis, that a change of physical activity is associated with a change of quality of life in physical and psychological area. A change in self-efficacy for functioning with multiple sclerosis leads to a change in physical area of quality of life and a change in self-efficacy for controlling multiple sclerosis is the strongest predictor of a change of quality of life. In conclusion, it may be stated that leisure time activities and non-formal education are associated with quality of life, contribute to improvement of its partial components depending on a type, frequency and intensity of an activity. Under certain circumstances, they increase the overall quality of life of an individual, which needs to be perceived as a tremendous potential of non-formal educational activity.

Literature

AITCHISON, C. (2000) *Young disabled people, leisure and everyday life: reviewing conventional definitions for leisure studies.* Annals of Leisure Research, Vol. 3, pp. 1–20.

American Therapeutic Association. [available https://www.atra-online.com/welcome/history, 2016-07-22].

ANDERSON, L. (2012) *Why leisure matters: Facilitating full inclusion.* Social Advocacy and System Changes Journal, Vol. 3 (1), p. 13.

AYVAZOGLU, N. R. – HYUN-KYOUNG, OH – KOZUB, F. (2006) *Explaining physical activity in children with visual impairments: A family systems approach.* Exceptional Children, Vol. 72 (2), pp. 235 – 248.

BARAN, J. – BARANIEWICZ, D. (2016) *On the contradictions and dilemmas arising from the evaluation of the quality of life of pupils with disabilities in the inclusive perspective.* International conference: Multidimensional Topography of the Quality of Life in Inclusive Education, 5th – 6th May 2016, Smolenice, Slovak Republic.

BENDIXEN, R. – SENESAC, C. – LOTT, D. – VANDENBORNE, K. (2012) *Participation and quality of life in children with Duchene muscular dystrophy using the International Classification of Functioning, Disability, and Health.* Health and Quality of Life Outcomes, Vol. 10, p. 9.

BERESFORD, B. – CLARCE, S. (2009) *Improving the wellbeing of disabled children and young people through improving access to positive and inclusive activities.* University of York.

BIZOVÁ, N. (2016) *Interaktionen zwischen Gleichaltrigen in inklusiven Freizeitaktivitäten.* In Teilhabe und Vielfalt: Herausforderungen einer Weltgesellschaft. Bad Heilbrunn: Verlag Julius Klinkhardt, pp. 388 – 398.

CLARKE, H. (2006) *Preventing Social Inclusion of Disabled Children and Their Families.* The University of Birmingham.

DAHAN-OLIEL, N. – SHIKAKO-THOMAS, K. – MAJNEMER, A. (2012) *Quality of life and leisure participation in children with neurodevelopmental disabilities: a thematic analysis of the literature.* Quality of Life Research, Vol. 21, pp. 427 – 439.

DĚDOVÁ, M. (2015) *Vnímanie sociálnej opory od spolužiakov a učiteľov v súvislosti so šikanujúcim správaním.* In BOZOGÁŇOVÁ, M. – KOPANIČÁKOVÁ, M. – VÝROST J. (eds.). *Sociálne procesy a osobnosť. Človek a spoločnosť.* Košice: Spoločenskovedný ústav SAV, pp. 115 – 121.

DĚDOVÁ, M. (2016) *Prežívanie strachu zo šikanovania v súvislosti s percepciou sociálnej opory od učiteľov a spolužiakov.* In MILLOVÁ, K. – SLEZÁČKOVÁ, A. – HUMPOLÍČEK, P. – SVOBODA M. (eds.). Sociální procesy a osobnost 2015. Brno: Masarykova univerzita, pp. 72 – 78.

DOLEŽALOVÁ J. – ONDRÁKOVÁ J. – NOWOSAD, I. (2011) *Kvalita života v kontextech vzdělávání.* Zielona Góra: Uniwersytet Zielonogórski.

ERATAY, E. (2013) *Effectiveness of leisure time activities program on social skills and behavioral problems in individuals with intellectual disabilities.* Educational Research and Reviews, Vol. 8 (16), pp. 1437 – 1448.

ERIKSSON, L. – GRANLUND, M. (2004) *Conceptions of participation in students with disabilities and persons in their close environment.* Journal of Developmental and Physical Disabilities, Vol.16 (3), pp. 229 – 245.

European Agency for Special Educational Needs and Inclusive Education (2015) European Hearing – Luxembourg Recommendations. Luxembourg. [available https://www.european-agency.org/country-information/united-kingdom-england/publications/en?page=1, 2016-07-22].

European Agency for Special Educational Needs and Inclusive Education (20011) Key Principles for Promoting Quality in Inclusive Education. Brussels. [available https://www.european-agency.org/country-information/united-kingdom-england/publications/en?page=2, 2016-07-22].

GARCIA-VILLAMISAR, D. A. – DATTILO, J. (2010) *Effects of a leisure program on quality of life and stress of individuals with ASD.* Journal of Intellectual Disability Research, Vol. 54 (7), pp. 611 – 619.

GOLD, D. – SHAW, A. – WOLFFE, K. (2010) *The social lives of Canadian youths with visual impairments.* Journal of Visual Impairment & Blindness, Vol. 104, pp. 431 – 443.

GRAHAM P. – STEVENSON J. – FLYNN D. (1997) *A new measure of health-related quality of life for children.* Psychology and Health, Vol. 12, pp. 655–665.

GÜLŞAH, S. – CAN, O. – GÖZAYDIN, G. (2011) *Does regular physical activity in children affect the quality of life?* Journal of Physical Education and Sport, Vol. 11 (1), pp. 70 – 74.

HEWETT, R. – DOUGLAS, G. – RAMLI, A. – KEILL, S. (2012*) Post-14 transitions – A survey of the social activity and social networking of blind and partially sighted young people: Technical Report.* Birmingham, University of Birmingham.

HUTZLER, Y. – CHACHAM-GUBER, A. – REITER, S. (2013) *Psychosocial effects of reverse-integrated basketball activity compared to separate and no physical activity in young people with physical disability.* Research in Developmental Disabilities, Vol. 34, pp. 579 – 587.

KASSING, G. (ed.) (2010) *Inclusive Recreation. Programs and Services for Diverse Population.* Champaign: Human Kinetics.

KEIL, S. – FRANKLIN, A. – CROFTS, K. – CLERY, L. AND COLE-HAMILTON, I. (2001) *The social life and leisure activities of blind and partially sighted children and young people aged 5 – 25 (research report from Shaping the Future survey).* London: RNIB.

KELLY, E. – KLAAS, S. – GARMA, S. – RUSSELL, F. – VOGEL, L. (2012) *Participation and quality of life among youth with spinal cord injury.* Journal of Pediatric Rehabilitation Medicine: An Interdisciplinary Approach, Vol. 5, pp. 315 – 325.

KING G. – LAW M. – HURLEY P. – HANNA S. – KERTOY M. ET AL. (2004), *Children's Assessment of Participation and Enjoyment (CAPE) and Preferences for Activities of Children (PAC).* San Antonio, TX: Harcourt Assessment, Inc.

KRATOCHVÍLOVÁ, E. (2010) *Pedagogika voľného času.* Bratislava: Veda.

LASY, K. E. – ALLENDER, S. E. – KREMER, P. J. – SILVA-SANIGORSKI, A. M. – MILLAR, L. M. – MOODIE, L. M. – MARHEWS, L. B. – MALAKELLIS, M. – SWINBURN, B.A. (2011) *Screen time and physical activity behaviors are associated with health-related quality of life in Australian adolescents.* Quality of Life Research, Vol. 21, pp. 1085 – 1099.

LONGMUIR, P. – BAR-OR, O. (2000) *Factors influencing the physical activity levels of youths with physical and sensory disabilities.* Adapted Physical Activity Quarterly, Vol. 17, pp. 40 – 53.

MCCONCEY, R. – DOWLING, S. – HASSAN, D. – MENKE, S. (2012) *Promoting social inclusion through Unified Sports for youth with intellectual disabilities: A five-nation study.* Journal of Intellectual Disability Research, Vol. 33 (1), s. 229 – 239.

MOTL, R.W. – MCAULEY, E. – WYNN, D. – SANDROFF, B. – SUH, Y. (2013) *Physical activity, self-efficacy, and health-related quality of life in persons with multiple sclerosis: analysis of associations between individual-level changes over one year.* Quality of Life Research, Vol. 22, pp. 253 – 261.

Národní institut dětí a mládeže: Patříte mezi nás? aneb Kdy se daří začleňování dětí s handicapem od oddílů a kroužků. O výsledcích výzkumu na téma: Klíčové faktory ovlivňující inkluzi dětí a mládeže se specifickými vzdělávacími potřebami do zájmového a neformálního vzdělávání. 2010. [available http://znv.nidv.cz/projekty /realizace-projektu/klice-pro-zivot/inkluze-deti-se-specialnimi-vzdelavacimi-potrebami, 2016-07-22].

National Recreation and Park Association (1999) Position Statement on Inclusion. [available http://www.nrpa.org/Search.aspx?mssearch=postition%20statement %20 on%20inclusion#/886933213d4728e3a69c16669f5ae67d, 2016-07-22].

NZEGWU, F. – DOOLEY, G. (2008) *Functionality and the Needs of Blind and Partially-Sighted Young People in the UK: A Survey of Young People, Parents, Educators and Mobility Specialists*. Hillfields: The Guide Dogs for the Blind Association.

SCHLEIEN, S. – GREEN, F. – STONE, CH. (2003) *Making friends within inclusive community recreation programs*. American Journal of Recreation Therapy, Vol. 2 (1), pp. 7 – 16.

SHANK, J. W. – COYLE, C.P. – BOYD, R. – KINNEY, W.B. A. (1996*) Classification scheme for therapeutic recreation research grounded in the rehabilitative sciences*. Therapeutic Recreation Journal, Vol. 30 (3), pp. 179 – 197.

SHIELDS, N. – SYNNOT, A. (2016) *Perceived barriers and facilitators to participation in physical activity for children with disability: a qualitative study*. BMC Pediatrics, open access.

SHIKAKO-THOMAS, K. – DAHAN-OLIEL, N. – SHEVELL, M. – LAW, M. – BIRNBAUM, R. – ROSENBAUM, P. – POULIN, CH. – MAJNEMER, A.(2012) *Play and be happy? Leisure participation and quality of life in school-aged children with cerebral palsy*. International Journal of Pediatrics, 7p.

STUART, E. M. – LIEBERMAN, L. – HAND, K.E. (2006) *Beliefs about physical activity among children who are visually impaired and their parents*. Journal of Visual Impairment and Blindness, Vol. 100 (4), 21p.

TSAI, E. – FUNG, L. (2009) *Parents' experiences and decisions on inclusive sport participation of their children with intellectual disabilities*. Adapted Physical Activity Quarterly, Vol. 26, pp. 151 – 171.

VANNER, E. A. – BLOCK, P. – CHRISTODOULOU, C. (2008) *Pilot study exploring quality of life and barriers to leisure-time physical activity in persons with moderate to severe multiple sclerosis*. Disability and Health Journal, Vol. 1, pp. 58 – 65.

WHO (1997) WHOQOL – Measuring Quality of Life.

5 Quality of Life of Pupils with Sensory Impairment in Formal Education

5.1 Introduction

The implementation of the principles of inclusion became a matter of interest of the Slovak professional and political public after the ratification of the UN treaty Convention on the Rights of Persons with Disabilities on 25th June 2010 (Announcement by the Ministry of Health of the Slovak Republic No. 317/2010 Coll. and 318/2010 Coll.). The effort of inclusive education is complete acceptance of individuals with disability, disturbance or endangerment and their integration to education community with a new quality of cooperation, in which heterogeneity is principally understood as normal (Lechta 2010). If individuals with impairment are integrated to education at a regular school, questions related to the quality of their life in the given school environment in comparison to individuals educated in a segregated, or selective type of special schools (further on SPS) arise. The emphasis is placed on their social engagement and complex inner and outer support with the intention to increase quality of life (further on QoL). The phenomenon of inclusion transcends the lines of educational policy and affects social systems (Political Guidelines for Inclusion in Education, Appendix 1, 2009).

The trend toward inclusion is documented in the global strategy of the World Health Organisation (further on WHO) and concretised in international reference classifications, which are useful for transdisciplinary communication through finding a common scientific language and formation of systemic solutions for improving social participation of persons with health impairment or another disadvantagedness. The International Classification of Functioning, Disability and Health (further on ICF) states a positive and negative determination of the components of QoL, because limitations connected to disability are mainly a social problem. According to the WHO, they are in a mutual interaction:

1. functional abilities and disability – a dynamic relationship between health conditions and contextual factors:
   a) body functions and structures – physiological systems and anatomic structures including muscle power, locomotion and mental functions (cognitive, emotional, conative processes);
   b) activity – in the sense of functionality of locomotion, transfer, care for oneself, communication and knowledge application;
   c) participation – in the sense of self-service, mobility, information exchange, establishment and maintenance of social relationships, homely life and care for others, education, work and occupation

with the level of economic independence, participation in social and civil life;

2. concurring factors:
   a) environmental factors – physical and social factors, attitudes of people;
   b) personal factors – individual's background and sociodemographic indicators such as gender, ethnicity, age, lifestyle, habits, coping with stress, etc.

We hold it important so that the indicators for QoL assessment contain components determined by the WHO. In a study aimed at the survey of QoL of pupils with hearing and visual impairment educated at regular and special schools, we selected a research tool that would map the given field and that would be suitable both for pupils with visual impairment and hearing impairment (Schalock et al. 2012) and for whose construction corresponds with the ICF components.

It is based on a definition by the WHO that defines QoL as a subjective category of perception, i.e. "an individual's perception of their position in life in the context of the culture and value systems in which they live and in relation to their goals, expectations, standards and concerns" (WHOQOL 1996). QoL is a multidimensional construct influenced by physical health, mental state, degree of autonomy or emotional richness and frequency of social relationships as well as environment features.

The construct of quality of life is based on individual perception and values, and an individual may use it while identifying support and services that they need for improvement of satisfaction with their life (Morgan 2009). QoL is changed according to individual values and in the course of time (Brown et al. 2003). Assessing QoL regards a complex measurement of physical, mental and social well-being, happiness, satisfaction and meaningfulness as they are perceived by an individual (Nagpal, Sell 1992). The issue of multidimensionality and complexity is shown mainly in the efforts to define QoL unanimously (Brown et al. 2009). The interest in QoL has been raised also in the Slovak educational circles, not excluding the field of inclusive education of pupils with disabilities (Dvořáčková 2012; Hlásna 2011; Jesenský 2007; Libigerová, Müllerová 2001; Novosad 2011; Požár 1999; Tokárová 2002; Vaďurová, Mühlpachr 2005 and others.).

According to Schalock et al. (2002), the understanding of QoL is useful for individuals with impairment for assessment of services or efficiency of intervention programs. Using the indicators of QoL it is possible to find areas of life that require improvement and consequently, efficient remedies can be taken (Schalock et al. 2010). Schippers (2010) considers the application of the multidimensional framework with several domains and a presupposed cross-cultural validity to be the basic criteria of the QoL research.

In some countries, there still exists an inappropriate behaviour toward individuals with impairment and a connection of their existence with lower QoL (Lyons 2010). According to Cummins (2001), persons living in a limited environment, including institutions, do not have to have an opportunity to discover a normal and broadly determined environment at all. Other authors (Albrecht et al. 2001; Devlieger et al. 2003) reached a conclusion that some persons with impairment, no matter the severity of their impairment, assess the quality of their life as good or even great. Such opposing findings emphasise that perception is a critical aspect of quality of life and as the researchers admitted, perception determines people's behaviour.

According to Amundson (2005), intact individuals believe that QoL of persons with impairment is low. It is a so-called anomaly of QoL including opposing findings: a standard measure of objective QoL and conflicting self-assessing reports of persons with impairments. Several studies present undetected differences in QoL in regard to the level of severity of impairment (Bach, Tilton 1994; Fuhrer et al. 1992; Nosek et al. 1995); others discovered that QoL is lower in relation to a more severe level of impairment (Menhert at al. 1990; Clayton, Shubon 1994; Lucas 2007). Findings that are more consistent can be found about the comparison of the period of impairment origination. The studies show (Uppal 2006) that the sooner an impairment is acquired, including congenital impairment, the higher QoL is. Studies that search for connections between QoL and severity of impairment present similarly strong connections between QoL and social factors such as employment and integration into the society. Even despite the fact that some categories of persons with disabilities (persons with severe impairment or those who live in rather inaccessible environments) have lower average QoL than the intact population; the overall average is much higher than persons without impairment would expect (Albrecht, Devlieger 1999).

5.2 Research Study Presentation

Our research intention was to find out about the quality of life of pupils with visual and hearing impairment whose education is carried out in regular and special schools, whether there exist significant differences in the values of QoL among the pupils with sensory impairment and to find out about possible impacts of statistical findings on empirical practice (Dolejš

2015). In our study, we focused on the rate of QoL in individual domains and overall QoL referring to a type of institution of education, type, degree and period of origination of the sensory impairment and we explored the relationships among them. We examined linear dependence among the indicators of QoL in regard to the domains of QoL, the strength of a relationship among the variables in basic populations of the respondents with sensory impairment and whether it is possible to predict potentially protective or inhibition factors based on the results (Gajdošíková Zeleiová, Bizová 2016).

Studies aimed at overall QoL of children/pupils often carry out their research with a general sample of school-age children/pupils. Several authors (Gilman et al. 2004; Brown et al. 1999; Green, Reid 1999; Griffin, Huebner 2000) consider the increase of QoL for a primary goal of every child/pupil and social intervention, including individuals with impairment. Studies applying QoL measurement tools related to health (HRQOL) show that children with unfavourable health conditions have worse results than their normally developing peers (Wake et al. 2003).

Research problem

Relatively fewer studies compare QoL of children with impairment to their intact peers. Measurement of QoL assessment carried out in this manner requires a universal tool that could be used for both groups of pupils. Discussing QoL of pupils with visual and hearing impairment majority of studies focus on the impact of the loss of sight or hearing on QoL (Streufert 2008; Gothwal 2009), or on efficiency of corrective aids (Vitale et al. 2000) that were intentionally used in intervention so that they improved communication and decreased limitations caused by the loss. Studies aimed at children with hearing impairment prove that these children have more social and behavioural problems than their peers do (Davis, Hind 1999; Eldik et al. 2004). The study of Gilman et al. (2004) reveals that young people with hearing impairment report lower life satisfaction in several domains of QoL in comparison to their intact peers.

Research sample

The research group consisted of 144 respondents with a sensory impairment aged 9-20 years old (average age 13.59; SD=2.15), including 60 girls and 84 boys, being educated by individual integration in regular primary schools [♀15, ♂21] and secondary schools [♀3, ♂10] or in the system of special education [♀42, ♂53] in Slovakia. Data were obtained by a combination of purposive sampling from a directory of the Institute of Information and Prognoses of Education after acquiring a written informed consent of parent/parents of a respondent and consent of school management. The structure of the research group was considered on the basis of competently selected criteria – a type of sensory impairment and a special or integrated way of schooling. There were 60 pupils with hearing impairment, including 34 with a hearing aid, at the same time 17 having a Cochlear implant. There were 84 respondents with visual impairment, including 40 using corrective glasses, at the same time 27 using a magnifying glass. Pupils with hearing impairment were represented in the following ratio: 60 % hard of hearing and 40 % deaf. Considering visual impairment there were 16 % of blind pupils, 64 % of purblind pupils and 20 % of pupils with the remains of sight, as stated in Table 1, in which the research sample is ar-

Tab. 1. Contingency data of the research sample with regard to the type of sensory impairment, degree, period of the impairment origination, way and grade of schooling

Impairment	Degree		School			Total
			SPS	PS	SS	
Visual	purblind	congenital	22	5	4	31
		acquired before 6th year of age	10	4	1	15
		acquired 6th year of age	8	0	0	8
		Total	40	9	5	54
	with remains of sight	congenital	6	3	2	11
		acquired before 6th year of age	3	1	0	4
		acquired 6th year of age	1	1	0	2
		Total	10	5	2	17
	blind	congenital	9	3	0	12
		acquired before 6th year of age	0	0	1	1
		Total	9	3	1	13
Hearing	hard of hearing	congenital	6	4	4	14
		acquired prelingually	10	6	0	16
		acquired postlingually	2	4	0	6
		Total	18	14	4	36
	deaf	congenital	14	4	1	19
		acquired prelingually	3	1	0	4
		acquired postlingually	1	0	0	1
		Total	18	5	1	24

ranged according to the period of origination of the sensory impairment. The research data were collected by the method of individual structured interview of researchers with respondents in 2013-14 and the method of scaling of personal results POS-CA in 2014-15 (Schalock et al. 2012).

Research tool

Since the attention in the research is focused on quality of life of pupils with visual and hearing impairment in regular and special schools, it was mainly the age and specific particularities of these pupils that were taken into consideration while selecting a tool appropriate for QoL measurement of the given group of respondents. For the measurement of the subjective assessment of QoL an adapted Personal Outcomes Scale for Children and Adolescents (further on POS-CA) by Schalock et al. (2012) was used. POS-CA assesses QoL of individuals aged 6 – 18 in eight domains described below and consists of 89 items assessing, on a 3-point Likert-type scale, the frequency of occurrence of a certain phenomenon and features (often – sometimes – never, a lot – some – none) or functionality of the occurrence (I can do it myself – I can do it with assistance – I cannot do it myself). In POS-CA assessment, self-assessment intersects with assessment by a direct observer; in our research, besides 144 respondents the assessment was carried out by 48 pedagogues who had the opportunity to acquaint with the respondents for the period of at least three months; however, a comparison is not a subject of the given study. The original tool (Schalock et al. 2012) consists of 8 domains represented by 48 items. Van Loon, Bernshausen, Löbler, Buchenau (2012) confirmed good reliability of the tool (Cronbach's alpha .81). Verifying individual items in two pre-researches (Gajdošíková Zeleiová, Dolejš 2015, Dolejš 2018) we modified the tool for the Slovak children and youth population, which consisted in semantic division of original items with a more detailed determination of variables. The inner consistency of the modified questionnaire including 89 items was increased (Cronbach's alpha .88) in comparison to the tool used in the pre-research. The data on reliability are provided in Table 2. The authors state Cronbach's alpha for individual domains between .60 and .70 (Van Loon et al. 2012).

Schalock et al. (2009) determine the scale of personal results by the factors of QoL, i.e. constructs of higher order such as independence, social participation and well-being, and by the domains of QoL, i.e. a group of factors defining multidimensionality of QoL, and by the indicators of QoL related to perception, experiencing and behaviour of a respondent. The authors of the tool divided the construct of QoL into three areas (Schalock et al. 2002):

1. basic domains of QoL like Personal development (further on PD), Self-determination, (further on SD), Interpersonal relations (further on IR), Social inclusion (further on SI), Rights (further on RI), Emotional well-being (further on EW), Physical well-being (further on PW), Material well-being (further on MW);
2. basic principles influencing QoL that concern needs of an individual, same for persons with impairment and intact persons – the need of independence, social participation and life well-being;
3. principles of application of QoL, which are principles of QoL used in order to increase personal well-being of persons with disability and to increase their effective control over possibilities in their environment, with regard to individual and culturally specific values, regardless the political situation.

The indicators of QoL in individual domains are, for example, status of education, abilities, adaptive behaviour in the domain personal development, choices, decisions, autonomy, self-control, personality goals in the domain self-determination, social environment, friendship, social activities, relationships in the domain interpersonal relations, integration into community, participation, social status, social support in the domain social inclusion, human rights such as respect, dignity, equality and lawful rights of approach, justice of process in the domain rights, protection and safety, positive experiences, satisfaction in the domain emotional well-being, health, style of boarding, rest, free time in the domain physical well-being, and financial state, accommodation, possession in the domain material well-being.

POS-CA measures subjective indicators of QoL (perceptional) as well as objective ones (life events); it is based on holistic approach to a person. As the authors state (Schalock et al. 2009), criteria for selection of a specific indicator reflect the needs of a respondent and the rate of their saturation in his/her life. The results may be used for the purposes of improvement of information or services mediation and they are relevant for various diagnostic groups as well as for intact persons. A provider of services may control the quality of services based on these results. The measurement is sensitive to ethical and culturally bound features of the domains and indicators of QoL, it includes the perspective of the system at macro-, mezzo- and micro- level. The scale POS-CA provides feedback about limits and possibilities of QoL and planning and orientation of a change of QoL.

Schalock (1997) discusses, in connection to QoL, the importance of reaching consensus about the basic dimensions of the quality of life of all people, including persons with impairment, and harmonising of the provision of services and support with prediction of basic dimensions of the quality of life connected to the development of support technology. The predictive ability of the research tool is confirmed not only by its good construction features, but also by several international studies in the field of inclusive education and psychology of persons with impairment (Van Loon et al. 2008, 2009, 2010, 2012; Claes et al. 2009, 2011; Brown at al. 2009; Schalock et al. 2002, 2010).

5.3 Methods and Data Analysis

Data were sorted and analysed in the programme SPSS® 20.0.0. Examining basic descriptive characteristics of the measured variables and inner consistency of the domains of QoL (Tab. 2) satisfactory conclusions were reached; the values of Cronbach's alpha show acceptable data between

Tab. 2. Correlation matrix of the domains of QoL POS-CA of respondents with sensory impairment and Cronbach's alpha of the domains of the adapted research tool POS-CA

Impairment (Person Correlations)		Personal development	Self-determination	Interpersonal relations	Social inclusion	Rights	Emotional well-being	Physical well-being	Material well-being
Cronbach`s alpha (Σ items)		.75 (17)	.69 (12)	.49 (10)	.75 (14)	.67 (6)	.64 (8)	.40 (9)	.62 (13)
Visual impairment	Personal development	1.000							
	Self-determination	.476*	1.000						
	Interpersonal relations	.236	.258	1.000					
	Social inclusion	.522**	.369	.079	1.000				
	Rights	.290	.172	.215	.190	1.000			
	Emotional well-being	.400*	.349	.300	.167	.540**	1.000		
	Physical well-being	.163	.277	.159	.080	.299	.363	1.000	
	Material well-being	.409*	.378	.130	.339	.236	.357	.229	1.000
Hearing impairment	Personal development	1.000							
	Self-determination	.579**	1.000						
	Interpersonal relations	-.167	.181	1.000					
	Social inclusion	.507**	.501**	-.005	1.000				
	Rights	.146	.407*	.245	.274	1.000			
	Emotional well-being	.158	.408*	.331	.303	.446*	1.000		
	Physical well-being	.298	.302	.038	.229	.139	.176	1.000	
	Material well-being	.495*	.255	-.037	.344	.289	.212	.197	1.000

* Correlation is significant at level of significance .05. ** .01 (two-sided testing)

.60 and .70, with the exception of the quality of interpersonal relationships and physical well-being. We were interested in the results of correlation analysis between the domains of QoL and individual indicators of QoL in the groups of respondents according to their sensory impairment. The results are presented in Table 2, where the existence of a linear relationship between the variables of QoL in the research group of respondents with visual or hearing impairment was confirmed. The partial correlation coefficients for individual domains of QoL and the observed variables from the indicators of QoL were quantified in exploration manner, while the variable impairment was controlled. Close relationships were brought together and the model was constructed with regard to the indicators of QoL (Figure 1, 2), without seeking to claim causal connections.

Our concern was to detect statistically significant differences among the QoL domains in various samples of subjects from the research group of pupils, stratified according to the type of education, type, degree and period of origination of the sensory impairment. For comparison, we used one-way analysis of variance ANOVA for independent selections after verifying homogeneity by F-test, consequently – if a significant difference among averages of individual groups was identified – we used post hoc Fisher's LSD test for determination of significant differences of QoL and for comparison of significance of values in individual domains. If the conditions for normal distribution were not met, we investigated the statistical significance of differences of QoL by Kruskal-Wallis test.

5.4 Results

Our research interest was to find out about the linear dependence among the QoL indicators with regard to the QoL domains, the strength of the relationship among the variables in research groups of respondents with sensory impairment and whether it is possible to predict life quality of pupils with sensory impairment in the environment of various types of schools and thus, to encourage their autonomous self-development. The way of schooling, i.e. education in a special type of schools or integrated type of regular schools moderately relates to the usage of corrective prosthetic aids. If a pupil with hearing impairment uses a hearing aid, their overall QoL is better if they are educated in a special primary schools. We used a linear regress model to explain the dependence r=.387 and the moderation effect, where the hearing aid is the predictor of higher QoL (R2=.144, p=.023, β=.379). On the other hand, Cochlear implant is a good predictor of higher QoL only if a pupil, who has it implanted, is educated in an individual type of integration at regular primary schools (r=.305) or secondary schools (r=.374). Regarding pupils with visual impairment, a relation between using a magnifying glass and higher QoL was confirmed only in education at secondary schools (r=.449) in an individual type of integration, however, moderation effect is insignificant.

Further, on we were interested whether there exist statistically significant differences among the QoL domains in various samples of subjects from the research group in connection to the way of education, type, degree and period of sensory impairment origination, and how they are different empirically. Significant differences were noted in Table 3 to 5 in descriptive characteristics. The data enable to answer the research questions related to QoL of the pupils with sensory impairment whose education takes place in regular and special schools. It was proved that better PW relates to pupils with visual impairment educated in the inclusive way (F=4.319, p=.007 at level α=.05). Regarding pupils with hearing impairment educated in the inclusive way, QoL scores significantly higher in SD (F=10.337, p=.005 at level α=.05), SI (F=7.613, p=.016 at level α=.05) and MW (F=12.328, p=.00 at level α=.05).

The ANOVA results indicate that in regard to the respondents with visual impairment, the type of education has a significant impact on QoL in PD, i.e. if they are educated in a SPS, they have higher social as well as practical competencies and efficiency connected to productivity in comparison to their peers in regular primary school (F=3.628, p=.41 at level α=.05). Similarly, a significantly higher level of QoL in SI (F=3.223, p=.036 at level α=.05) is in favour of pupils with visual impairment educated in SPS in comparison to pupils educated in regular primary schools.

At stratification of the group according to the degree of visual impairment it was conformed that the depth of visual impairment influences QoL in SI (F=7.109, p=.014 for purblind vs. with remains of sight, p=.001 for purblind vs. blind at level α=.05). A significant influence of the degree of hearing impairment on QoL was confirmed only in selected domains such as SD (F=12.303, p=.003 at level α=.05), IR (F=2.488, p=.028 at level α=.05), SI (F=3.299, p=.012 at level α=.05) and PW (F=3.223, p=.041 at level α=.05). Cochlear implant as a predictor of better QoL has been mentioned already above.

The fact whether a respondent acquired the visual impairment prenatally (congenital) or postnatally (after the 6th year of age) is not critical

Tab. 3. Comparison of averages of values of QoL in individual domains and in total in groups of respondents with visual and hearing impairment educated in different types of school

Visual impairment	Primary school			Special primary school			Secondary school		
	Average	SD	Median	Average	SD	Median	Average	SD	Median
Personal development	27.92	5.10	28.00	29.80[a]	3.68	30.00	30.13	3.60	30.50
Self-determination	18.40	3.19	19.00	17.69	3.06	18.00	22.50[ab]	1.41	23.00
Interpersonal relations	11.44	1.85	12.00	11.32	2.95	12.00	11.75	1.49	11.50
Social inclusion	9.60	4.36	8.00	12.07[a]	5.35	12.00	14.00[a]	3.12	15.00
Rights	9.60	1.63	10.00	9.52	2.14	10.00	9.50	2.93	10.50
Emotional well-being	12.00	1.78	12.00	11.96	2.63	12.00	13.38	2.39	14.00
Physical well-being	16.04[b]	2.15	16.00	14.37	2.77	14.00	15.75	2.25	15.00
Material well-being	20.68	3.35	21.00	19.75	4.30	20.00	23.25[b]	1.67	23.00
QoL	123.52[c]	16.95	128.00	130.23[c]	16.99	131.00	107.00	15.16	105.00
Hearing impairment	Primary school			Special primary school			Secondary school		
	Average	SD	Median	Average	SD	Median	Average	SD	Median
Personal development	30.32	4.09	32.00	28.67	3.33	29.00	32.14[b]	2.27	33.00
Self-determination	17.64[b]	3.67	17.50	15.04	3.57	15.00	20.71[ab]	3.04	22.00
Interpersonal relations	11.77	2.25	12.00	11.40	2.69	12.00	11.29	1.80	12.00
Social inclusion	13.36[b]	4.25	14.00	10.73	4.23	11.00	16.57[b]	4.50	18.00
Rights	9.68	1.70	10.00	9.15	2.27	10.00	9.71	1.98	10.00
Emotional well-being	11.95	2.10	12.50	11.45	2.88	11.00	14.00[b]	2.24	14.00
Physical well-being	15.86[b]	2.27	16.00	14.55	2.57	14.00	16.00	2.89	16.00
Material well-being	22.32[b]	2.73	23.00	18.55	3.73	19.00	22.86[b]	2.79	24.00
QoL	120.41	16.81	118.50	127.31[a]	12.69	128.00	127.00	10.68	124.00

p<.05
a – the value is statistically significantly higher towards the respondents from primary schools at level α=.05
b – the value is statistically significantly higher towards the respondents from special primary schools at level α=.05
c – the value is statistically significantly higher towards the respondents from secondary schools at level α=.05

for QoL either in the individual domains or totally. With the probability of 95 %, no significant differences were discovered in QoL in regard to the period of visual impairment origination. The lowest average score of QoL was discovered in respondents with visual impairment acquired after the 6th year of age [AM=120.14; SD=16.73; Med(x)=123.5], the highest score in respondents who acquired the visual impairment up to the 6th year of age [AM=130.00; SD=16.98; Med(x)=131]. Respondents with congenital visual impairment display the score of QoL in the middle of the two given groups [AM=127.060; SD=18.20; Med(x)=130]. Either the differences, however, are not statistically significant in the individual QoL dimensions or totally; nevertheless, the differences are empirically logical.

Emotional well-being [EW] is more significant in respondents with prenatal hearing impairment than in those who acquired the impairment after acquisition of mother tongue (F=2.729, p=.036 at level α=.05). On the contrary, respondents with postlingual hearing impairment are significantly better equipped with material well-being [MW] than the prelingually impaired (F=2.729, p=.036 at level α=.05).

Tab. 4. Comparison of averages of values of QoL in individual domains and in total in groups of respondents with visual and hearing impairment of different degree

Visual impairment	Purblind			With remains of sight			Blind		
	Average	SD	Median	Average	SD	Median	Average	SD	Median
Personal development	29.58	4.27	30.00	28.95	3.61	29.00	29.06	3.91	29.00
Self-determination	17.96	3.35	18.00	19.05	3.34	20.00	18.35	2.55	18.00
Interpersonal relations	11.13	2.67	12.00	12.00	2.92	13.00	11.76	2.02	12.00
Social inclusion	12.86 [bc]	5.18	13.00	9.74	4.58	8.00	8.59	3.43	8.00
Rights	9.24	2.36	10.00	10.11	1.15	10.00	10.18	1.24	10.00
Emotional well-being	11.68	2.71	12.00	12.89	1.85	13.00	12.82	1.33	13.00
Physical well-being	15.01	2.90	15.00	14.74	2.60	15.00	14.35	1.73	14.00
Material well-being	20.26	4.27	20.50	19.63	3.32	19.00	20.71	3.95	21.00
QoL	130.04 [c]	17.83	131.00	125.68	14.77	128.00	115.29	17.01	115.00

Hearing impairment	Hard of hearing			Deaf			With Cochlear implant		
	Average	SD	Median	Average	SD	Median	Average	SD	Median
Personal development	29.73	3.39	30.00	28.94	3.88	29.00	30.63 [de]	2.99	31.00
Self-determination	17.17 [e]	3.59	17.50	14.89	4.07	14.50	16.54	5.07	17.00
Interpersonal relations	12.02 [e]	2.25	13.00	10.78	2.67	11.00	10.75	2.42	11.50
Social inclusion	13.06 [e]	4.18	12.50	10.36	4.69	11.00	12.29	6.01	12.50
Rights	9.46	2.25	10.00	9.17	1.92	10.00	9.21	2.00	10.00
Emotional well-being	12.00	2.86	12.00	11.53	2.52	11.00	11.67	2.63	11.00
Physical well-being	15.52 [e]	2.40	15.00	14.33	2.68	14.00	16.08 [de]	3.06	15.50
Material well-being	19.77	4.18	20.00	20.06	3.48	20.00	21.75 [de]	3.04	22.50
QoL	126.08	13.41	127.00	124.67	14.72	124.00	125.08	11.70	122.50

p<.05

a – the value is statistically significantly higher towards the purblind respondents at level α=.05

b – the value is statistically significantly higher towards the respondents with remains of sight at level α=.05

c – the value is statistically significantly higher towards the blind respondents at level α=.05

d – the value is statistically significantly higher towards the hard of hearing respondents at level α=.05

e – the value is statistically significantly higher towards the deaf respondents at level α=.05

Tables 3 to 5 present a set of results after the variance analysis aimed at examination of the influence of independent variables, such as the way of schooling (special, inclusive), degree and period of origination of sensory impairment on the QoL domains in groups of respondents with visual or hearing impairment.

At nominal level, we compared the rate of overall QoL with respect to the type of sensory impairment and the type of education, however, the differences did not prove to be statistically significant when good agreement was tested (Chi^2=.295). At cardinal level, we compared the overall rate of QoL and the rate in individual domains of respondents with different type of sensory impairment, and similarly, statistical significant differences were not proved, besides the value of QoL in SD (t=4.127, p=.000 at level α=.05), where the respondents with visual impairment scored significantly higher. The comparison in terms of gender at the cardinal level shows that boys score in the overall QoL significantly higher than girls (t=-2.102, p=.037

Tab. 5. Comparison of average values of QoL in individual domains and in total in groups of respondents with visual and hearing impairment that originated in different period

Visual impairment	Congenital			Acquired before 6th year of age			Acquired after 6th year of age		
	Average	SD	Median	Average	SD	Median	Average	SD	Median
Personal development	29.69	3.84	30.00	28.43	4.67	29.00	29.43	4.36	29.50
Self-determination	18.44	3.23	19.00	18.09	3.13	18.00	17.29	3.47	18.50
Interpersonal relations	11.35	2.47	12.00	11.61	2.73	12.00	11.14	3.37	12.00
Social inclusion	11.23	4.84	10.00	12.35	5.42	12.00	12.57	6.07	15.50
Rights	9.54	2.14	10.00	9.61	1.85	10.00	9.43	2.24	10.00
Emotional well-being	12.42	2.33	13.00	11.43	2.52	12.00	11.36	2.76	11.00
Physical well-being	14.62	2.87	14.00	15.26	2.54	16.00	15.43	1.83	15.00
Material well-being	20.30	4.39	21.00	20.17	3.42	20.00	19.93	3.29	20.00
QoL	127.06	18.20	130.00	130.78	16.98	131.00	120.14	16.73	123.50
Hearing impairment	Congenital			Acquired prelingually			Acquired postlingually		
	Average	SD	Median	Average	SD	Median	Average	SD	Median
Personal development	29.15	3.54	30.00	29.41	3.89	30.00	31.00	2.83	31.00
Self-determination	15.92	4.38	16.00	16.14	3.40	16.00	18.29	2.29	18.00
Interpersonal relations	11.58	2.50	12.00	11.45	2.68	13.00	11.00	1.91	11.00
Social inclusion	11.58	5.19	12.00	11.69	3.24	12.00	15.00	4.24	16.00
Rights	9.42	2.15	10.00	9.17	2.14	9.00	9.43	1.90	10.00
Emotional well-being	12.29[b]	2.34	12.00	11.41	3.16	12.00	10.00	2.45	9.00
Physical well-being	14.67	2.62	14.00	15.41	2.29	15.00	15.71	3.35	15.00
Material well-being	20.15	3.60	20.00	18.83	4.31	20.00	22.57[a]	2.30	23.00
QoL	125.75	14.44	126.00	123.10	13.31	125.00	133.43[a]	10.81	138.00

p<.05

a – the value is statistically significantly higher towards the respondents with prelingually acquired hearing impairment at level α=.05

b – the value is statistically significantly higher towards the respondents with postlingually acquired hearing impairment at level α=.05

at level α=.05). However, a detailed analysis reveals that the difference is significant only in the domains of EW (t=-2.403, p=.018 at level α=.05) and MW (t=-2.522, p=.013 at level α=.05) at normal distribution of values in the groups.

Based of bivariate statistics, strong statistical connections in linear relationships between the QoL domains and QoL indicators were assembled in the research group of respondents with visual and hearing impairment and empirical models presented in Fig. 1 and 2 were constructed. However, these may not actually indicate direct causality and moderating bonds.

5.5 Discussion

The outcomes of the study (Tab. 2, Fig. 1, 2) showed that in both groups of respondents with sensory impairment personal development connected to cognitive, social or practical competences [PD] moderately correlates

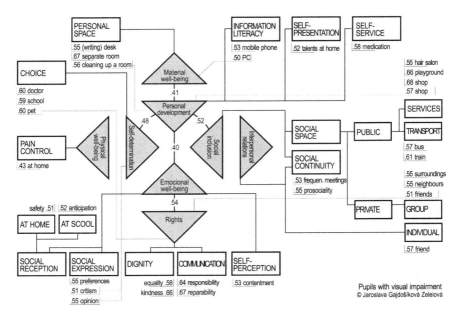

Fig. 1. Model of positively significant partial correlations with the size of effect r>0.5 in respondents with visual impairment (n=84), p<0.05 at level α=.05

with the ability of autonomous decision-making, self-control and self-determination connected to setting of goals and integration of values [SD]. The direct relationship between personal development [PD] and the rate of social inclusion expressed by integration in a given community and participation in its life or by the rate of social support from the environment [SI] is equally moderate. For both groups with sensory impairment, personal development [PD] is relatively moderately strongly associated with material possibilities, possession and usage of various technological equipment [MW]. Interestingly, there is a relatively strong correlation between the perception of human and legal rights, such as self-experience with equality, justice and respect [RI] and emotional well-being [EW] expressing the emotional component of self-concept and self-acceptance. The statistical findings correspond with experience.

While assembling individual indicators, differences in the area of personal development [PD] were discovered; it is less differentiated in pupils with hearing impairment, which can be associated with formation of a different self-concept (Potměšil 2000; Procházková et al. 2007; Lejska 2003). In pupils with visual impairment, it is connected not only to the possibilities of obtaining and sorting information, but also to an increased need of self-

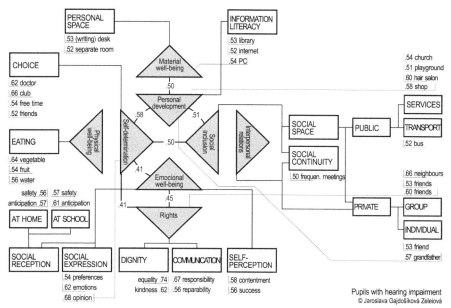

Fig. 2. Model of positively significant partial correlations with the size of effect r>0.5 in respondents with hearing impairment (n=60), p<0.05 at level α=.05

presentation of own abilities in home environment, which could indicate lack of appreciation in their primary family.

After the analysis of corrective aids on QoL it may be stated that in the group of pupils with hearing impairment educated in SPS, the usage of a hearing aid is a predictor of better QoL; the Cochlear implant predicts higher QoL only if a pupil is educated in an integrated way, which is also confirmed by Leonhardt (2013a).

After stratification of pupils according to the type of education (Tab. 3) and type, degree (Tab. 4) and period of origination of sensory impairment (Tab. 5), it was found out that the rate of better physical well-being [FW] is perceived by the integrated pupils independently of the type of impairment and it is associated with a subjective image of a healthy man. Only in the group of pupils with hearing impairment, a relation was found with a diet containing enough fruits and vegetables; in regard to pupils with visual impairment the consciousness of health is associated with caution and pain avoidance.

Based on significant indicators (Tab. 3), the empirical significance of the importance of education of pupils with visual impairment in a selective way in SPS is proved in regard to the impact on their personal development

[PD] and social inclusion [SI]. However, it does not relate to pupils with hearing impairment; they demonstrate a higher rate of social inclusion [SI] if integrated in regular types of schools. Pupils with hearing impairment benefit more from individual integration, because they are forced to enter interaction with their peers despite the communication barriers (Jariabková et al. 2013). The level of language competencies, methods of education and support of a family proved to be important factors of school success (Leonhardt 2013b).

A connection of school success with personal qualities like friendliness, conscientiousness and openness was found out in individuals with visual impairment (Klinkosz et al. 2006). Agran et al. (2007) add that the ability of independent decision-making can be limited in individuals with visual impairment and connected to dependence on other people; however, it was not proved in our study, on the contrary – self-determination [SD] connected to the possibilities of choice is higher in pupils with hearing impairment if integrated in regular school.

While interpreting the given difference, where the selective education of pupils with visual impairment has a positive impact on personal development [PD] connected to learning, information access, the ability of orientation in social and intrapsychic space in the sense of autonomy and a positive impact on social inclusion [SI], we can ground the interpretation in the research on psycho-social particularities of individuals with visual impairment (Hamadová et al. 2007; Lang et al. 2008; Požár 2007; Shirley 1997; Vágnerová 2004). The particularities of their cognitive as well as social learning require timely and primary intervention; therefore, we accentuate the importance of specific approach in education to these pupils mainly at the beginnings of their schooling and orientation in the socio-cultural world.

Different indicators were reached by Bártlová (Bártlová, Matulay 2009), who addressed the issue of QoL of pupils with visual impairment in the area of their adaptation to special and regular school. Based on the QoL findings in the area of adaptation, independent from a type of school, she states that it is lower in pupils with visual impairment than in the intact population. Compared to integrated pupils, the pupils from SPS were more submissive, which can be later demonstrated in some social situations as decreased self-esteem associated with the lack of interactions with the intact population. The author points out to the positive of integrated education of pupils with visual impairment. The author did not find clear differences between the integrated pupils and the pupils educated at SPS in the area of emotionality, majority of individuals reached weak or dissatisfactory level. In the area of hostility, she presents results in favour of SPS pupils. The reason of increased hostility in integrated pupils is interpreted as a consequence of their increased need of self-assertion among the intact peers within a classroom.

The study brought similar results in regard to pupils with visual as well as hearing impairment at the level of their social inclusion [SI] (Tab. 4) according to the degree of impairment: the less severe the impairment is, the higher the participation of respondents in social life connected to the ability of assembling and utilisation of public services is. Better emotional well-being [EW] is observed in pupils born with hearing impairment in comparison to those who acquired the impairment postnatally (Tab. 5). At the same time, it seems, in regard to significantly higher achievement of material well-being [MW] by individuals with postlingually acquired impairment, that they could be endowed with affluence by their surroundings in a hypercompensation manner (Tab. 5), while we presuppose a reason of inadequate compassion among other things. It is understandable that these individuals achieve higher QoL in total, since their speech barrier is milder.

The structure of ICF offers a socio-medical approach to the solution of serious issues of QoL. Taking into consideration the principles assumed by the classification, we measured the possibilities and limits of QoL with the impact on active school life of pupils with impairment. Our examination of QoL of pupils with sensory impairment was based mainly on two indicators of functionality according to ICF – activity, participation and environmental factors. In subcategories of activity and participation, we understood cognitive, emotional, social and behavioural engagement of a person with disability in the direction from the person to the environment. It regards stimulation acting outwardly from a respondent to the environment, while in the subcategories of the environmental factors we observed interactions of the environment with an individual with disability and possibilities or opportunities that they are offered by the environment from the outside towards them. Both dynamics of indicators are implanted in the QoL domains in POS-CA (Fig. 1, 2). For further researches, we recommend to add a dimension of spiritual well-being connected to meaningfulness, in accordance with the definition of health by WHO (1998) as a dynamic state of complete physical, mental, spiritual and social well-being (Dolejš, Gajdošíková Zeleiová 2015).

We are aware of the limits that the design of the presented research brings. The study does not have a longitudinal design, in which QoL of individuals would be observed across developmental particularities. We analysed only the subjective perception of respondents, without correlation with the assessment of 48 pedagogues, who had the opportunity to acquaint with respondent/s for the period of at least three months. At the same time, the representation of respondents from primary and secondary schools and respondents with a different period of origination of the impairment was not proportional. It could not have been influenced due to limited directories of the Institute of Information and Prognosis of Education at the Slovak Centre of Scientific and Technical Information and due to parents' willingness to cooperate. Therefore, the conclusions of the study are perceived with carefulness, without claiming direct causal connections. Despite the limitations of the research findings, we draw a conclusion that there exist specific significant differences of QoL in respondents with visual impairment in regard to the type of impairment as well as the way of education.

5.6 Conclusion

The research was focused on differences in the overall QoL and QoL in its individual dimensions among pupils with visual and hearing impairment educated in regular schools and special schools. Based on the research findings, it can be stated that no significant differences were proved between the groups of pupils with visual and hearing impairment in the overall QoL. However, a partial QoL domain expressed in the ability of self-determination as an ability to express own needs and choices, is significantly higher in pupils with visual impairment in comparison to pupils with hearing impairment. Examination of bivariate relationships in selected groups of respondents among the QoL domains and QoL indicators led to discovery of empirical differences that were formulated into a model of conjugated relationships. For further understanding of QoL in pupils with sensory impairment, it is necessary to examine moderation and causal bonds, which can reveal deeper connections; or transcultural comparison that would show particularities of national systems of education.

Literature

AGRAN, M. – HONG, S. – BLANKENSHIP, K. (2007) *Promoting the self-determination of students with visual impairments. Reducing the gap between knowledge and practice.* Journal of Visual Impairment and Blindness 101, pp. 453 – 464.

ALBRECHT, G. L. – DEVLIEGER, P. J. (1999) *The disability paradox: high quality of life against all odds.* Social Science and Medicine 48, 977–988.

ALBRECHT, G.L. – SEELMAN, K.D. – BURY, M. (2001) *Handbook of Disability Studies.* London, New Delhi: Sage Publications.

AMUNDSON, R. (2005) *Disability, ideology, and quality of life: a bias in biomedical ethics.* In WASSERMAN, D. – BICKENBACH, J. – WACHBROIT, R. (eds.): Quality of life and human difference. Cambridge UK: Cambridge University Press, pp. 101 – 124.

BACH, J. R. – TILTON, M. C. (1994) *Life satisfaction and well-being measures in ventilator assisted individuals with traumatic tetraplegia.* Archives of Physical Medicine and Rehabilitation 75, pp. 626 – 634.

BÁRTLOVÁ, S. – MATULAY, S. (2009) *Sociologie zdraví, nemoci a rodiny.* Martin: Vydavateľstvo Osveta.

BROWN, W. H. – ODOM, S. I. – ZERCHER, C. (1999) *Ecobehavioral assessment in early childhood programs: A portrait of preschool Inclusion.* Journal of Special Education 33, pp. 138 – 153.

BROWN, I. – BROWN, R. I. (2003) *Quality of Life and disability. An approach for community practitioners.* London: Jessica Kingsley Publishers.

BROWN, R. I. – SCHALOCK, R. L. – BROWN, I. (2009) *Quality of Life: Its application to persons with intellectual disabilities and their families – Introduction and overview.* Journal of Policy & Practice in Intellectual Disabilities 6, pp. 2 – 6.

CLAES, C. – VAN HOVE, G. – VAN LOON, J. – VANEVELDE, A, S. – SCHALOCK, R. L. (2009) *Eight principles for assessing quality of life-related personal outcomes.* Social Indicators Research 29, pp. 25 – 39.

CLAES, C. – VAN HOVE, G. – VANDEVELDE, S. – VAN LOON, J. – SCHALOCK, R. L. (2011) *The influence of supports strategies, environmental factors, and client characteristics on quality of life-related personal outcomes.* Research in Developmental Disabilities 33, pp. 96 – 103.

CLAYTON, K. S. – SHUBON, R. A. (1994) *Factors associated with the quality of life of long term spinal cord injured persons.* Archives of Physical Medicine and Rehabilitation 75, pp. 633 – 638.

CUMMINS, R.A. (2001) *Living with support in the community: Predictors of satisfaction of life.* Mental Retardation and Developmental Disabilities Research Reviews 7, pp. 99 – 104.

DAVIS, A. – HIND, S. (1999) *The impact of hearing impairment: A global health problem.* International Journal of Pediatric Otorhinolaryngology 49, pp. 51 – 54.

DEVLIEGER, P. – RUSCH, F. – PFEIFFER, D. (2003) *Rethinking disability. The emergence of new definitions, concepts and communities.* Antwerpen/Apeldoorn: Garant.

DOLEJŠ, V. (2015) *Kvalita života žiakov s postihnutím v základných školách* [Dizertačná práca]. Trnava, Trnavská univerzita.

DOLEJŠ, V. (2018) *Kvalita života žiakov so zmyslovým postihnutím v bežných a špeciálnych školách.* In LECHTA, V. ŠUHAJDOVÁ I. (eds). Koncept inkluzívnej edukácie v sociálno-pedagogických bádaniach. Typi Universitatis Tyrnaviensis, VEDA, pp. 126-152.

DVOŘÁČKOVÁ, D. (2012) *Kvalita života seniorů v domovech pro seniory.* Praha: Grada.

ELDIK, T. V. – TREFFERA, D. A. – VEERMAN, J. W. – VERHULST, F. C. (2004) *Mental health problems of deaf dutch children as indicated by parent´s responses to the child behavior checklist.* American Annals of the Dead 148, pp. 390 – 395.

FUHRER, M. J. – RINTALA, D. H. – HART, K. A. – CLERMAN, R. – YOUNG, M. E. (1992) *Relationship of life satisfaction to impairment, disability, and handicap among persons with spinal cord injury living in the community.* Archives of Physical Medicine and Rehabilitation 73, pp. 552 – 557.

GAJDOŠÍKOVÁ ZELEIOVÁ, J. – BIZOVÁ, N. (2016) *Quality of Life of Pupils with Sensory Impairment Educated in Ordinary and Special Schools.* In 3rd International Multidisciplinary Scientific Conference on Social Sciences and Arts SGEM 2016. Book 1 Vol. 1, pp. 1015-1022.

GAJDOŠÍKOVÁ ZELEIOVÁ, J. – DOLEJŠ, V. (2015) *Lebensqualität der Schüler mit Sinnesbeeinträchtigungen.* In LEONHARDT, A. – MÜLLER, K. – TRUCKENBRODT, T. (eds.). Die UN-Behindertenrechtskonvention und ihre Umsetzung. Beiträge zur Interkulturellen und International vergleichenden Heil- und Sonderpädagogik. Bad Heilbrunn, Verlag Julius Klinkhardt KG, pp. 468 – 476.

GILMAN, R. – EASTERBROOKS, S. R. – FREY, M. (2004) *A preliminary study of multidimensional life satisfaction among deaf/hard of hearing youth across environmental settings.* Social Indicators Research 66, pp. 143 – 164.

GOTHWAL, V. K. – WRIGHT, T. A. – LAMOUREUX E. L. – PESUDOVS, K. (2009) *Rasch analysis of the quality of life and vision function questionnaire.* Optometry and vision science 86, pp. 836 – 844.

GREEN, C. W. – REID, D. H. (1999) *A behavioral approach to identifying sources of happiness and unhappiness among individuals with profound multiple disabilitties.* Behavioral Modification 23, pp. 280 – 293.

GRIFFIN, M. D. – HUEBNER, E. S. (2000) *Multidimensional life satisfaction reports of middle school students with serious emotional disturbance.* Journal of Psychoeducational Assessment 18, pp. 280 – 293.

HAMADOVÁ, P. – KVĚTOŇOVÁ, L. – NOVÁKOVÁ, Z. (2007) *Oftalmopedie.* Brno, Paido.

HLÁSNA, S. (2011) *Sociálna klíma triedy a kvalita života žiaka v triede.* Bratislava, Lingua.

International Classification of Functioning, Disability and Health. World Health Organization (2001) Geneva, WHO Library Cataloguing-in-Publication Data.

JESENSKÝ, J. ET AL. (2007) *Prolegomena systému tyflorehabilitace, metodiky tyflorehabilitačních výcviků a přípravy rehabilitačně-edukačních pracovníků tyflopedického spektra.* Praha, Univerzita Jana Amose Komenského.

JARIABKOVÁ, K. – GROMA, M. – HÓKOVÁ, T. (2013) *Vnímanie úspechu a jeho determinanty úspešnými ľuďmi so zrakovým, sluchovým a mentálnym postihnutím.* Efeta otvor sa 23, pp. 4 – 9.

KLINKOSZ, W. – SEKOWSKI, A. – BRAMBRING, M. (2006) *Academic achievement and personality in university students who are visually impaired.* Journal of Visual Impairment and Blindness 100, pp. 666 – 675.

LANG, M. – HOFER, U. – BEYER, F. (2008) *Didaktik des Unterrichts mit blinden und hochgradig sehbehinderten Schullerinennen und Schulern.* Grundlagen. Stuttgart, Kohlhammer.

LECHTA, V. ET AL. (2010) *Základy inkluzivní pedagogiky.* Praha, Portál.

LEJSKA, M. (2003) *Poruchy verbální komunikace a foniatrie.* Brno, Paido.

LEONHARDT, A. (2013a) *Aplikácia inklúzie žiakov so sluchovým postihnutím v Nemecku.* In LECHTA, V. (ed.). Inkluzívna pedagogika a jej komponenty. Trnava, Typi Universitas Tyrnaviensis, pp. 176 – 185.

LEONHARDT, A. (2013b) *Reflection of Inclusive Education of Children with Hearing Disability.* In LECHTA, V. – KUDLÁČOVÁ, B. (eds.). Reflection of inclusive education of the 21st century in correlative scientific fields. Frankfurt: Peter Lang, pp. 113 – 118.

LIBIGEROVÁ, E. – MÜLLEROVÁ, H. (2001) *Posuzování kvality života v medicíně.* Česká a slovenská psychiatrie 97, pp. 183 – 186.

LUCAS, R. (2007) *Adaptation and the set-point model of subjective well-being.* Current Directions in Psychological Science 16, pp. 75 – 79.

LYONS, G. (2010) *Quality of Life for persons with intellectual disabilities.* In KOBER, R. (ed.). Enhancing the Quality of Life of people with intellectual disabilities: From theory to practice, New York: Springer, pp. 73 – 125.

MENHERT, T. – KRAUS, H. H. – NADLER, R. – BOYD, M. (1990) *Correlates of life satisfaction in those with disabling conditions.* Rehabilitation Psychology 35, pp. 3 – 17.

MORGAN, S. L. (2009) *Adaptive behavioral, self-determination, and quality of life for student with severe disabilities in inclusive and self-contained placements.* United States: ProQuest Umi Dissertation Publishing.

NAGPAL, R. – SELL, H. (1992) *Assessment of Subjective Well-being.* New Delhi: World Health Organization Regional Office in South-East Asia.

NOSEK, M. – FUHREHE, M. – POTTER, C. (1995) *Life satisfaction of people with physical disabilities: relationship to personal assistance, disability status, and handicap.* Rehabilitation Psychology 40, pp. 191 – 202.

NOVOSAD, L. (2011) *Tělesné postižení jako fenomén i životní realita.* Praha, Portál.

Oznámenie Ministerstva zahraničných vecí Slovenskej republiky č. 317/2010 Z. z. – Dohovor o právach osôb so zdravotným postihnutím.

Oznámenie Ministerstva zahraničných vecí Slovenskej republiky č. 318/2010 Z. z. – Opčný protokol k Dohovoru o právach osôb so zdravotným postihnutím.

Policy Guidelines on Inclusion in Education. United Nations Educational, Scientific and Cultural Organization, Paris, 2009, ED-2009/WS/31.

POTMĚSIL, M. (2000) Úvodní stati k výchově a vzdělávání sluchově postižených. Praha, Fortuna.

POŽÁR, L. (1999) Školská integrácia a kvalita života postihnutých. Psychológia a patopsychológia 34, pp. 195 – 201.

POŽÁR, L. (2007) Základy psychológie ľudí s postihnutím. Trnava, Typi Universitas Tyrnaviensis.

PROCHÁZKOVÁ, V. – VYSUČEK, P. (2007) Jak komunikovat s neslyšícím klientem. Praha, Vzdělávací institut ochrany dětí.

SCHALOCK, R. (1997) Quality of life. Application to persons with disabilities. Washington, American Association on Mental Retardation.

SCHALOCK, R. L. – CLAES, C. – VAN HOVE, G. – VAN LOON, J. – VANDEVELDE, S. (2009) Quality of Life Measurement in the Field of Intellectual Disabilities: Eight Principles for Assessing Quality of Life-Related Personal Outcomes. Social Indicators Research 98(1), pp. 61 – 72.

SCHALOCK, R. – VAN LOON, J. – MOONEN, L. – MOSTERT, R. – CLAES, C. (2012) Personal Outcomes Scale for Children and Adolescents POS-CA. Gent, Stichting Arduin.

SCHALOCK, R. – VERDUGO, M. A. (2002) Handbook on Quality of Life for human service practitioners. Washington DC: American Association on Mental Retardation.

SCHALOCK ROBERT L. – KEITH KENNETH D. – VERDUGO MIGUEL Á. – GÓMEZ LAURA E. (2010) Quality of Life Model Development and Use in the Field of Intellectual Disability. In KOBER R. (ed.). Enhancing the Quality of Life of people with intellectual disabilities: From theory to practice. New York: Springer, pp. 17 – 18.

SCHIPPERS, A. (2010) Quality of life in Disability Studies. Medische antropologie 22, pp. 277 – 288.

SHIRLEY, T. (1997) The characteristics of visually impaired children with multiple disabilities. [Vyhľadané 5. 11. 2014 na http://www.ebenezer-enhs.edu.hk/web_doc/visually_impaired_children_with_multiple_disabilities.htm].

STREUFERT, M. A. (2008) Quality of life measure for adolescents and children with hearing loss. Washington university school of medicine. [2012-06-05 http://digitalcommons.wustl.edu/cgi/viewcontent.cgi?article=1476&context=pacs_capstones].

The World Health Organization Quality of Life assessment (1996) What quality of life? World Health Forum. 17(4), pp. 354 – 356.

TOKÁROVÁ, A. (2002) K metodologickým otázkam výskumu a hodnotenia kvality života. In Kvalita života. V kontextoch globalizácie a výkonovej spoločnosti. Prešov, FF PU [Vyhľadané 18. 5. 2012 na http://www.ff.unipo.sk/kvdsp/download/ Zbrnk/ ZbornkKZvPrsv2002.pdf].

UPPAL, S. (2006) *Impact of the timing, type and severity of disability on the subjective well-being of individuals with disabilities.* Social Science and Medicine 63, pp. 525 – 539.

VAĎUROVÁ, H. – MÜHLPACHR, P. (2005) *Kvalita života. Teoretická metodologická východiska.* Brno, Masarykova univerzita.

VÁGNEROVÁ, M. (2004) *Psychopatologie pro pomáhající profese.* Praha, Portál.

VAN LOON, J. – BERNSHAUSEN, G. – LÖBLER, F. – BUCHENAU, M. (2012) *Personal Outcomes Scale POS. Individuelle Qualität des Lebens.* St. George, BoD.

VAN LOON, J. – CLAES, C. – VANDEVELDE, S. – VAN HOVE, G. – SCHALOCK, R. L. (2010). *Assessing Individual Support Needs to Enhance Personal Outcomes.* Exceptionality 18(4), pp. 193 – 202.

VAN LOON, J. – VAN HOVE, G. – SCHALOCK, R. L. – CLAES, C. (2008). *Personal Outcomes Scale: A Scale to Assess an Individual's Quality of Life.* Middelburg, Stichting Arduin and Gent, University of Gent.

VAN LOON, J. – VAN HOVE, G. – SCHALOCK, R. L. – CLAES, C. (2009). *Personal Outcomes Scale: Administration and Standardization Manual.* Middelburg, Stichting Arduin and Gent, University of Gent.

VITALE, S. – SCHEIN, O. D. – MEINERT, C. L. – STEINBERG, E. P. (2000) *The Refractive Status and Vision Profile: A questionnaire to measure vision-related quality of life in person with refractive error.* Ophthalmology 109, pp. 1529 – 1539.

WAKE, M. – SALMOVE, I. – REDDIHOUGH, D. (2003) *Health status of Australian children with mild to severe cerebral palsy: cross-sectional survey using the Child health questionnaire.* Developmental Medicine and Child Neurology 45, pp. 194 – 199.

6 Quality of Life of Pupils with Visual Impairment

6.1 Introduction

In Poland, visually impaired students can be enrolled in one of the three educational systems: segregated, integrated, and inclusive. Polish schools are modelled on the solutions adopted in Hamburg. The first principles of organizing classes in mass schools for the pupils qualified for special education were created by the Ministry of Education in 1983. However, detailed regulations for organizing care and instruction for pupils affected by disabilities at the preschool and school level were first laid in a 1993 decision of the Ministry of Education (Bogucka, Kościelska 1996). The ministerial regulations issued in 2010 strongly emphasize the implementation of the principle of individualized work with the pupils, supporting the pupils and the teachers, flexibility and adequacy of all actions adapted to the pupils' needs, and personal partnership for the sake of the pupils (Dziennik Ustaw 2010 no. 228 point 1489).

At present, the inclusive education project is promoted as the one built on a unique premise. What is assumed is that it is not the child that requires modification and adaptation to the school system, but, on the contrary, the school and the system must be modified to meet the individual needs of all children, both the typically and non-typically developing ones. The rule of heterogeneity is promoted, stating that children in one class constitute one group with diversified individual needs. This process is still in progress, as not only the education must change, but mainly teachers' approach to pupils with disabilities. They must not be seen as those who need to adapt to the proposed forms of education, but as those to whom the forms of education must be adjusted. Another direction of change should target the perception of disabled children by their peers; it remains one of the elementary educational tasks, therefore the existing educational system does not qualify as inclusive yet, but it is by all means integrative. There are but few studies on the subjective well-being and sociometric status of visually impaired children and youth enrolled in the integrative system. The studies reveal that, despite not being entirely satisfied with their situation, such children are neither rejected (the examined groups included some sociometric stars), nor isolated. The author of this paper can confirm, basing on her own research, that crucial factors in subjective well-being in a school class are the personality and the social competences of the examined students with visual impairments (Konarska 2013, pp. 122 – 132).

The Main Statistical Office provides the following data for 2013: in the school year 2012/13, primary and secondary regular schools were attended by 4745 pupils with vision loss and visual impairments, while special schools were attended by four times fewer pupils with visual impairments. The 2011 collective report of the Polish Association of the Blind states that from among 4369 children and teenagers enrolled in all types of schools, 73 % (3202 students) attended regular schools, 20 % (863 students) – schools for the visually impaired, and 7 % (304 students) – other special schools (Łukasiak, Oleksiak 2011). The number of blind and visually impaired students at different levels of education has been approximately the same for several years. Out of all the students qualified for special education, the visually impaired pupils of elementary (regular and special) schools constitute a mere 0.3 %, while pupils with mild intellectual disabilities constitute around 42 % of all children with disabilities. Such quantitative disproportion makes the visually impaired pupils a low-representation group of disabled students. This, in turn, affects the degree of interest in the visually impaired persons e.g. when it comes to removing architectonic barriers and adapting the surroundings to their needs. Very infrequently are those needs considered at the design stage or in the adaptation works that should make the surroundings friendly to persons affected by disabilities.

6.2 Quality of Life in Scientific Research

The term "quality of life" was introduced into scientific terminology in the 1960s, and it was defined as an individual's material possessions (possessing wealth, owning a house, having a high standard of living). With time, the notion expanded to include spiritual values, such as freedom, health, education, or happiness (Rostowska 2009, p. 15). This approach allows assigning a high rank to individuals' potential and resources, which those individuals are encouraged to use.

While evaluating the quality of life, attention is paid to all values that create its uniqueness. Focus can be placed on a certain style of behaviour or action, or a characteristic manner of experiencing situations.

Quality of life is presented as a multidimensional construct, which includes various areas of an individual's activity. Considering the fact that a person may express satisfaction in every area of their life, it is recommended to take into account multiple spheres of life and to concentrate on all of their aspects, not only on the selected ones. Neglecting some of the needs may cause considerable damage to young people's quality of life, their development, or health. Thus it must be emphasized that quality of life is a dynamic process, changing over longer periods of time, especially in adolescence, when evaluation of the quality of life will be related to the expectations and experiences linked to the biological age, social maturity, and psychological needs (Oleś 2002, pp. 72 – 73).

Both in Poland and worldwide, more and more studies are conducted into the quality of life of persons affected by illness or disability (Ostrzyżek 2002; Mayou, Bryant 1987; Palak, Lewicka, Bujnowska 2006). That kind of investigation is aimed at disclosing to what extent particular dysfunctions of the organism and their nature affect the level of the quality of life. Re-searchers also attempt to identify other factors that determine a given lev-el of quality of life in persons affected by illness or disability (Fox, Kilvert 2003). Such research facilitates organizing the rehabilitation process so that the disabled persons experience their life inconveniences to the least possible extent.

Quality of life evaluation with respect to health issues includes those ar-eas of everyday activity that may be affected by the dysfunction experien-ced by the individual. Therefore, usually several aspects are considered:
- Functional well-being, understood as the ability to actively engage one-self in everyday situations connected with work and leisure;
- Physical well-being, including the experienced discomforts;
- Emotional well-being, which expresses the positive or negative emotio-nal states;
- Abilities connected with maintaining good relations and contacts with family members;
- Social functioning, including the satisfaction brought by fulfilling va-rious social roles;
- Satisfaction with the medical treatment;
- The intimate sphere (Peterman, Cella 2000, p. 492).

Research on the quality of life is not conducted with equal intensity among persons with different disabilities. There are few studies referring to persons with visual impairments. Visual dysfunctions considerably influ-ence the quality of life, since it is assumed that over 80 % of all information is obtained via the visual channel. At present, the most acute discomfort ex-perienced by persons with visual impairments is the difficulties in or com-plete lack of spatial orientation. Any other inconvenience can be signifi-cantly alleviated with the help of modern technologies, especially IT. Still, it remains a fact that achieving a subjective sense of comfort by visually impaired persons is difficult, especially in such areas as: using sources of information, functioning in the social life, own activity, or leisure activities

(Oleś 2002, p. 10). Those hindrances may be reflected in at least four dimensions of an individual's functioning, i.e. their physical state, psychological state, social situation, and material conditions. Therefore, in the theoretical research a need arose to introduce a new notion, namely "health-related quality of life". It is defined as a functional effect of the illness and the treatment, as experienced by the very person affected by illness or disability (Okła, Steuden 2007, p. 6).

Persons with visual impairments are also exposed to traumatic and uncomfortable experiences linked to the process of treatment and rehabilitation. Long treatment in medical facilities, staying away from one's friends and family, the experienced pain, but also the progress and results of rehabilitation diverging from the patient's expectations may negatively influence their sense of the quality of life (Oleś 2002). Yet other markers of quality of life are characteristic of persons experiencing vision loss, as the elementary problem in their case is the acceptance of their condition (Casten, Rovner 2008). Usually, visual impairments cause lack of independence, and sentence the person to complete reliance on other people's help. The awareness of being dependent on others may negatively affect the individual's sense of well-being and self-worth.

Dimensions of the Quality of Life

In the evaluation of health-related quality of life, the following dimensions are potentially significant:
1. physical well-being, including the experienced discomforts, e.g. pain or nausea;
2. functional well-being, including the ability to participate in everyday professional and leisure activities; it also includes the ability to care for oneself (self-service) or deal with everyday tasks, functional self-reliance, and the ability to make choices;
3. emotional well-being, including positive and negative emotional states; it also comprises the sense of inner strength and life energy, sense of purpose in life, life satisfaction, self-satisfaction, and self-esteem;
4. familial well-being, or the ability to maintain good relations and contact with family members;
5. social functioning, which denotes the ability to participate in social activities and to fulfil social roles, as well as to feel satisfaction because of it; the social dimension includes such aspects as: social interactions, sense of security, empathy, extrovert behaviours, and social participation;

6. treatment satisfaction, including financial issues; financial issues belong to the material dimension of the quality of life, which can also cover personal possessions, such as a mobile phone or a computer;

7. sex and intimacy, including the issues connected with the perception of one's body;

The overall sense of quality of life can be expressed in terms of one category, reflecting the perceived average quality of life, or as a sum of all the above-mentioned partial categories, reflecting particular dimensions.

Evaluation of the quality of life is also conducted to examine the cognitive functioning, social stigmatization, and the spiritual sphere (Oleś, Steuden, Toczołowski 2002, p. 41). Because of the psychological aspects of life, which may be related to the sense of the quality of life, another aspect is also worth considering, namely the early development of emotional-cognitive social mechanisms, on which the self-image and self-esteem will be based in the future.

6.3 The Sense of Self-worth

The sense of self-worth is not only the key that enables opening the unconscious potential hidden in every person and developing that person's self-assurance. It is a crucial element of the inner life of an individual, which conditions health, satisfaction, and good functioning in almost every sphere of life. Thus, it also contributes to the level of the quality of life.

The sense of self-worth is the first stage of developing self-esteem and plays a significant role in interpersonal relations. Without a developed sense of self-worth, an individual feels lost in the surrounding world, lacks proper orientation towards social requirements, and lack the ability to care for their own needs (McKay, Fanning 2004, p. 11). At the age of three, a child develops a unique, particular "self". Using the pronoun "I" is a confirmation of this phenomenon. Owing to its existence, the processes occurring internally, experienced by a person, can be differentiated from the processes occurring in the outer world, dependent on other people or the forces of nature. Undoubtedly, the conception of one's "self" is a precondition of proper orientation, but also a source of motivational tension. In turn, changes in self-evaluation condition activate the increase in motivational tension. Not only objects are evaluated but also one's own persona. Thus, the sense of self-worth means the awareness of one's own position on the evaluation scale (Konarska 2002, p. 50). Additionally, the sense of self-worth can be described as a subjective, dynamic component of an individual's persona, not as a static, tangible entity, easily observable and measurable. It begins to develop at the moment in time when one experiences the feeling of being separate, the awareness of one's individual existence as a person (Lindenfield 1995, pp. 17, 25). A positive perception of oneself triggers the formation of such features as the sense of self-dignity, self-assurance, ability to perceive oneself realistically, and the ability to conduct efficient evaluation of relations with others, which results in good adaptation skills. In turn, lowered perception of oneself triggers a sense of inadequacy and inferiority, lack of faith in one's own potential, a strong reaction to criticism, and limited chances of initiating satisfactory interpersonal relations. Therefore, the above-described elements will be a manifestation of a poorer psychosocial preparation (Konarska 2002, pp. 101-108). At the same time, they determine the level of the quality of life.

Self-esteem

The sense of self-esteem is one of the first emotional-social experiences that organize the world with respect to the ranking of importance of its living and non-living elements, and with respect to the priority assigned to particular needs. In the emerging individual system of values, a person occupies a special position, both as an object of evaluation by others, and as an object of self-evaluation. In this way self-esteem is shaped – an inherent part of a person's self-image.

The cognitive components and the judgmental-evaluative concepts of oneself are strongly related and mutually dependent. People's visualization of their appearance, physical features, capabilities, ability to undertake various tasks, fulfilment of social roles, and interpersonal relations determine evaluation of oneself in a large part. It turns out that a positive attitude towards one's "self" in all its dimensions is conducive to successful adaptation of the human being to the environment, and conditions satisfaction with oneself and the sense of high quality of life. The self-esteem influences the cognitive processes, motivation, and behaviour, perception of the closest relations, aspiration and life plans, and the choice of values (Kulas 1986, p. 32).

Disability may constitute a factor, which in itself lowers both the sense of self-worth and the self-esteem built on its basis. Both these personality components set the level and direction of social activity. A child with no disabilities faces no limitations (apart from the natural, developmental ones) in the realization of its activity. Such a child usually proceeds to the next stages of development in environments in which most children in the given culture live; thus their social experience is enriched in a natural way. On the other hand, children with disabilities are not always ready to undertake the customary social roles, even when they have reached the appropriate age. They may function in the same environment, yet their participation in their peers' life, and the type and frequency of activities is usually not as rich as other children's participation. The interpersonal relations they enter are also different, and they rarely experience being distinguished, or at least approved of, by those who evaluate them. In this situation, developing the sense of self-worth, which is supposed to be the foundation for the emerging system of self-evaluation, is not just a challenging task, but also one that is emotionally unattractive. At the preschool age, when developmental differences between children are still quite natural, the problem is not that serious: in building the knowledge and judgments of oneself, the parents' attitude and opinion is of much greater importance than the child's experiences outside the family (Konarska 2013, p. 92). In late childhood and adolescence, contacts with peers and other acquaintances, or even strangers, become the basis of the acquisition of knowledge about oneself. In turn, the quality of that knowledge influences the subjective sense of the quality of life.

Interpersonal Relations

Both shaping the sense of self-worth and setting the level of self-evaluation occur through social interaction; therefore, interpersonal relations, their frequency, and the emotional attitude towards others become one of the most prominent indicators of the quality of life. The experience gained in this way and the connected emotions set the range of social activity, and at the same time affect the level of satisfaction with life, oneself, and others, who offer help when necessary. The special time in life when we turn towards others is adolescence. However, children who did not obtain a confirmation of their importance in the previous stages of development, who did not experience satisfaction and security in contacts with another person, cannot, and will not, leave the relatively safe family circle for the sake of entering broader relations with peers and other social communities. Staying in the shadow of peers does not facilitate the efforts to realize the set goals, or even hinders the initiative of any own activity. It thus diminishes the level of ambition and the belief in one's causative power. Such a state lowers the mood, and psychological well-being, which is one of the indicators of the quality of life, is practically unattainable. Dissatisfaction with one's coexistence in a social group indirectly contributes to the resignation from any efforts towards improving one's education or professional qualifications, and from achieving such level of social life that safeguards a financially comfortable life. The sense of financial security is another factor that guarantees emotional stability and thus improves the quality of life. The self-evaluation which is in agreement with one's possibilities, which includes both potentials and limitations, facilitates realizing the rehabilitation plans, and enables accepting life challenges, which, in turn, provides satisfaction and increase the quality of life.

6.4 The Research Study Presentation

Quality of life evaluation was conducted in a group of students aged 10-20 enrolled in integrative schools; a control group included students of special schools. The experimental group was divided into two age subgroups: 10-15 and 16-20. The 10-15 group consisted of 36 students and the 16-20 group – of 30 students, which in total gives 66 respondents. Moreover, for each subgroup, the same number of students in the same age attending special schools were selected. Thus, 132 students were examined. It seems that without the control group, the results would not yield practical conclusions: not with respect to the sensibility of integrative education, which is undisputable, but considering the changes in educational practice directed at that group of students who display disturbing symptoms in evaluation of selected aspects of the quality of life.

6.5 Methods and Data analysis

To elicit information on the levels of the sense of quality of life among the respondents, the Quality of Life Questionnaire (QQL) was administered in its version for the visually impaired; it was delivered to the researchers by the Slovak colleagues. QQL – typhlo examines the subjective sense of the quality of life in the social, functional, and material areas.

Additionally, on the initiative of the Polish project executor, a psychologist by trade, two other tests were administered a metric psychological test, examining the quality of life: Psychological Scales Measuring Quality of Life, adapted by Z. Uchnast, and the Rosenberg Self-Esteem Scale – SES. A hypothesis was made that there is a correlation between the level of the quality of life and the level of self-esteem in students with visual impairments. This correlation was examined by means of Pearson's correlation coefficient r. Psychological Scales Measuring Quality of Life adapted by Z. Uchnast consists of four subscales, which investigate degrees of well-being, sense of purpose in life, life satisfaction, and self-satisfaction. The scale is built of 22 statements concerning well-being, sense of purpose in life, and life satisfaction, and 7 closed questions referring to self-satisfaction. Statements 1-22 are evaluated on the scale from 1 to 7: 1 – completely false; 2 – somewhat false; 3 – slightly false; 4 – neither true nor false; 5 – slightly true; 6 – somewhat true; 7 – completely true. In turn, self-satisfaction was measured on the 1 to 5 scale: 1 – never; 2 – rarely; 3 – sometimes; 4 – quite often; 5 – often. The data were interpreted using the key, which is an inherent element of the presented scale (Uchnast 2007).

To elicit information on self-esteem of the visually impaired students, the Rosenberg Self-Esteem Scale SES in its Polish version was used. The questionnaire contains 10 diagnostic statements, of which 5 express positive attitudes towards oneself, and the other 5 – negative attitude. The respondents indicate to what degree they agree with the statements by giving answers on a four-point scale: 1 – strongly agree; 2 – agree; 3 – disagree; 4 – strongly disagree. A respondent chooses one answer according to their agreement or disagreement with the statement. "The research shows that the Polish version is a highly reliable (Cronbach's alpha .81-.83), and theoretically valid instrument" (Łaguna, Lachowicz-Tabaczek, Dzwonkowska 2007).

6.6 Results and Discussion

The quality of life in the social area appears to be at a good level and increases with age both among the special education students and among the integrated education students (Tab. 1).

Tab. 1. Quality of life of the students surveyed - the social area

	Students surveyed											
Selected aspects of social area	% in integration						% in special education					
	Often		Sometimes		Never		Often		Sometimes		Never	
	Age 10-15	Age 16-20	Age 10-15	Age 16-20	Age 10-15	Age 16-20	Age 10-15	Age 16-20	Age 10-15	Age 16-20	Age 10-15	Age 16-20
Social interactions	41	40	48	60	11	0	38	50	50	50	12	0
Sense of security and empathy	34	26.7	58	70	8	3.3	33	66.7	59	33.3	8	0
Extrovert behaviour	26	16.7	70	63.3	4	20	43	63.3	52	30	5	6.7
Social participation	23	36.7	51	53.3	26	10	32	66.7	50	20	18	13.3

The youth enrolled in the integrated education become less spontaneous with age. It is visible in the decrease in the number of answers "often" and the noticeable increase in the number of answers "sometimes" with respect to social interactions, sense of security, and social participation." The number of extrovert behaviours decreases with age. All these changes may be evidence of growing control over one's behaviour with age, and since social participation and empathy increase, it may be concluded that the observed changes are positive, contribute to the improvement in the quality of life, and the respondents become progressively better integrated with the society.

Such conclusions cannot be drawn about the youth enrolled in special education (Tab. 2, 3). Even though with age the number of answers "often" increases in all social life categories, the answers "sometimes" indicate a visibly lessened sense of security and empathy, and lower social participation. It may indicate uncritical attitude towards oneself in some of the students aged 16-20, especially that they definitely reject the answer

Tab. 2. Quality of life of the students surveyed - the functional area

	Students surveyed											
	% in integration						% in special education					
	Often		Sometimes		Never		Often		Sometimes		Never	
	Age 10-15	Age 16-20	Age 10-15	Age 16-20	Age 10-15	Age 16-20	Age 10-15	Age 16-20	Age 10-15	Age 16-20	Age 10-15	Age 16-20
Self-service	85	98.9	13	1.1	2	0	76	98	20	2	4	0
Self-reliance	57	95	25	1.3	17	3.7	42	81.6	41	12.3	17	6.1
Dealing with everyday tasks	57	78.9	31	20	12	11.1	39	71.1	47	22.2	14	6.7
Making choices	70	71.7	22	12.7	8	15.6	65	88.9	26	7.2	9	3.9

Tab. 3. Material aspect of quality of life of the students surveyed

	Students surveyed											
	% in integration						% in special education					
	Often		Sometimes		Never		Often		Sometimes		Never	
	Age 10-15	Age 16-20	Age 10-15	Age 16-20	Age 10-15	Age 16-20	Age 10-15	Age 16-20	Age 10-15	Age 16-20	Age 10-15	Age 16-20
Ownership	39	3.3	54	66.7	7	30	37	3.3	58	56.7	5	40

"never" with respect to social interactions, sense of security, and empathy. They also observe very few extrovert behaviours (6.7 %), which are behaviours oriented towards other persons, and declare low participation in social life (13.3 %).

In the functional area, there is a clearly observable increase in all examined competences with age; thus, it can be concluded that the students surveyed are self-reliant and resourceful, although slight advantage is visible on the side of the integrative students.

With respect to the material conditions, the integrative schools student´s are in a somewhat better situation, but all respondents estimate their material well-being to be at a medium level.

Measurement of the psychological aspects creating the quality of life indicates that the sense of low quality of life is a marginal phenomenon in both age groups: 10 – 15 and 16 – 20. In both groups, most respondents estimate their level of the quality of life as average, although it is visibly lower in the case of special education students.

Among the students enrolled in special education, in each age group 13 students claim that their quality of life is high. That number does not change with age. Among the students of the integrative system, such a high degree of quality of life is declared by 6 pupils aged 10 – 15 and 5 pupils aged 16 – 20 (Tab. 4).

Tab. 4. Quality of life in "Psychological Scales Measuring Quality of Life"

Students surveyed											
N students in integration						N students in special education					
Low		Average		High		Low		Average		High	
Age 10-15	Age 16-20	Age 10-15	Age 16-20	Age 10-15	Age 16-20	Age 10-15	Age 16-20	Age 10-15	Age 16-20	Age 10-15	Age 16-20
5	4	25	21	6	5	4	3	19	14	13	13

Probably this result determined the distribution of means for psychological aspects of the quality of life, as higher results were obtained from special schools' students in both age groups (Tab. 5).

Tab. 5. The average of "Psychological Scales Measuring Quality of Life"

The average	Students surveyed	
	Integrated education	Special education
Age 10-15	149.1	156.4
Age 16-20	111.3	128.2

It is worth mentioning that in both types of education, evaluation of the quality of life lowers with age. It is likely that psychological maturing enables a more objective evaluation of the elements that create the subjective sense of quality of life. Children and youth enrolled in special education seem to fare better than students of the integrative system do: at least 3 out of 4 subscales measuring the psychological aspect of life yielded higher results than in the case of education students. However, that may be because of the fact that the scales refer to well-being, life satisfaction, and self-satisfaction. These subjective impressions are effects of social experience, which is not as rich as in the case of integrative students because of the limitations imposed by the special school environment. Special schools offer the sense of security, which translates to satisfaction and well-being. Further research on self-esteem reveals that special school students display high self-esteem, which even increases with age. It may mean that they feel comfortable in their partially isolated environment, and this environment sets the norms of social evaluation, according to which self-esteem is built (Tab. 6).

One of the dimensions examined while investigating the psychological aspects of the quality of life was the sense of self-satisfaction, which is reflected in the level of self-esteem. Thus, it may be suspected that high self-esteem will be positively correlated with high quality of life. To test this hypothesis, the respondents were examined using the Rosenberg Self-Esteem Scale SES. Table 6 presents the results of that examination.

Tab. 6. Level of self-esteem in The Rosenberg Self-Esteem Scale SES

Students surveyed											
N students in integration						N students in special education					
Low		Average		High		Low		Average		High	
Age 10-15	Age 16-20	Age 10-15	Age 16-20	Age 10-15	Age 16-20	Age 10-15	Age 16-20	Age 10-15	Age 16-20	Age 10-15	Age 16-20
1	4	24	22	11	4	1	1	23	19	12	10

In both groups of respondents, the integrated education and the special education students, and in both age groups, the dominant level of self-esteem is the average one. That level of self-esteem is clearly lowered in the group of older students of the integrated education, and only slightly lowered in the older group of special school´s students. It may indicate growing self-criticism, which is much higher in the integrated education. A large number of respondents classify themselves as persons with high self-esteem, especially those attending special schools, in both age groups. This result heightens the arithmetic mean for self-esteem, which is presented in table 7.

Tab. 7. The average of the Rosenberg Self-Esteem Scale SES

The arithmetic mean of the results	Students surveyed	
	Integrated education	Special education
Age 10-15	25.1	30.5
Age 16-20	24.8	28.7

If it is a fact that the level of quality of life and the level of self-esteem are mutually dependent, then the results of the "Psychological Scales Measuring Quality of Life" and "The Rosenberg Self-Esteem Scale" should correlate positively. To test this hypothesis, Pearson's correlation coefficient (r) was used. The results are presented in tables 8 and 9.

Tab. 8. The interdependence of quality of life and level of self-esteem

Age 10-15	Integrated education	Special education
Self-esteem	Quality of life	Quality of life
	r = 0.12	r = 0.17

Tab. 9. The interdependence of quality of life and level of self-esteem

Age 16-20	Integrated education	Special education
Self-esteem	Quality of life	Quality of life
	r = 0.64	r = 0.78

The numbers in table 8 reveal that there is little difference between the obtained correlations in both investigated sets of respondents. For children enrolled in integrated education the strength of correlation between the quality of life and self-esteem is r = 0.12, while for students of special schools it is r = 0.17. Thus in both sets the coefficient value is at a statistically significant level. According to Guilford's (1964) list of r- values, for the integrated education students the correlation is statistically significant, while for the control set it is statistically meaningful.

The results for the 16 – 20 age group also indicate a small difference between the obtained correlations. For the youth enrolled in integrated education, the strength of correlation between the quality of life and self-esteem is r = 0.64, while for the special schools students of the same age it is r = 0.78. Thus in both cases the coefficient reaches the statistically significant value. Following Guilford (1964), the correlation is statistically significant for the integrated education set, and statistically meaningful for the control set.

Taking into consideration the sign (+) of the correlation, the directly proportionate interdependence between variables is observed, i.e. high values of one variable will co-occur with high values of the other variable.

Therefore, it may be concluded that the level of self-esteem conditions the level of the quality of life.

6.7 Conclusion

The aim of the conducted research was to establish the level of subjectively perceived quality of life of visually impaired children and youth, enrolled in the integrated education in Poland. The research was conducted within an international project; all researchers used the same research questionnaire QQL in its version for persons with visual impairment. On the initiative of the research coordinator (a specialist in psychology and special pedagogy), the same questionnaire survey was administered in a group of students of special schools, which enabled a comparison of integrated education and special education students with respect to factors shaping the quality of life. Further, a Psychological Scales Measuring Quality of Life by Uchnast, and The Rosenberg Self-Esteem Scale – SES were used. Moreover, correlation between self-esteem and quality of life was postulated, and the hypothesis was tested. In addition, a multi-aspectual examination of the factors shaping the quality of life enabled a deepened analysis of the relation between the quality of life and the respondents' life and study environment.

Conclusions from the research are as follows:

1. The results of the QQL survey reveal that the quality of life in the social area is at a satisfactory level and increases with age, both among the integration students and special school´s students. However, with age, integrated education students tend to display more empathetic behaviours and greater social participation, while the results of the special education students reveal a clearly observable decrease in the sense

of security and empathy, and diminishing social participation. Thus, it may be deduced that integrated education students are better adapted to life in the society than special education students, therefore they may declare a higher level of quality of life.

2. The QQL survey reveals that in the functional area, competences in all examined skills increase with age. It may be deduced that the youth in the examined sample are self-reliant and resourceful, although the integrated education students fare slightly better in this respect.

3. The material area investigation by QQL is less informative, as financial means of the respondents in fact depend on the financial status of their parents and the respondents are unable to alter that situation. However, generally the obtained results indicate average satisfaction with the material situation.

4. Applying psychological tests provided more information on the factors shaping the quality of life. Examination by means of the "Psychological Scales Measuring Quality of Life" reveals that most respondents declare the average level of quality of life, although it is visibly lower in the case of special education pupils. It is noteworthy that in both educational systems the perceived quality of life lowers with age. It may be a result of maturing and developing greater self-criticism and criticism towards the world. Yet among the special education students, who declared a high level of the quality of life, this declaration is maintained regardless of age. The obtained results call for further, more detailed research to account for the observed situation.

5. Interdependence between the levels of quality of life and self-esteem (measured with Rosenberg SES) was hypothesized. The results show that such interdependence is a fact and the correlation is positive, i.e. the subjective perception of the quality of life is higher when self-esteem is higher; the opposite interdependence also occurs. The calculated correlation values are statistically significant.

6. The conducted study also brings practical conclusions. Obviously, it is recommendable to continue the research into the quality of life as perceived by children and youth with disabilities who function in different environments. Yet, it would be even more beneficial to include in this research psychologists, who possess a well-developed methodology and thus have the possibility to identify the dimensions that shape the quality of life more thoroughly and to establish correlations between them. Thus, judging from the presented research only, we realize that appropriate self-esteem must be built carefully, by gradual increase in the sense of self-worth in the process of personality development. Since

the process is long-lasting, and progresses within the context of socialization, it is recommendable to accustom children with disabilities to the conditions that they will face in their adult life, that is, in full social integration.

Literature

BOGUCKA, J. – KOŚCIELSKA, M. (1996) *Wychowanie i nauczanie integracyjne. Nowe doświadczenia.* Warszawa: PWN.

CASTEN, R. – ROVNER, B. (2008) *Depression in age-related macular degeneration.* Journal of Visual Impairment & Blindness, Vol. 102 no. 10.

FOX, C. – KILVERT, A. (2003) *Intensive education for lifestyle change in diabetes.* BMJ, Vol. 327.

GUILFORD, J. P. (1964) *Podstawowe metody statystyczne w psychologii i pedagogice.* (original title: Fundamental statistics in psychology and education). Warszawa: PWN.

KONARSKA, J. (2002) *Psychospołeczne korelaty poczucia sensu życia a niepełnosprawność.* Mysłowice: Wyd. GWSP.

KONARSKA, J. (2013) *Rozwój i wychowanie rehabilitujące dziecka niewidzącego w okresie późnego dzieciństwa i adolescencji.* Kraków: Wyd. UP.

KULAS, H. (1986) *Samoocena młodzieży.* Warszawa: WSiP.

LINDENFIELD, G. (1995) *Poczucie własnej wartości.* Łódź: Wydawnictwo "Ravi".

ŁAGUNA, M. – LACHOWICZ-TABACZEK, K. – DZWONKOWSKA, I. (2007) Skala samooceny SES Morrisa Rosenberga – polska adaptacja metody (The Rosenberg Self-Esteem Scale: Polish adaptation of the scale) *Psychologia Społeczna* Vol. 2, pp. 164 – 176.

ŁUKASIAK, K. – OLEKSIAK, E. (2011) Osoby niewidome i niedowidzące. In *Zbiorczy raport z diagnozy świadczonych usług z zakresu rehabilitacji społecznej dla osób niepełnosprawnych w Polsce.* Warszawa. www.koalicjaon.org.pl (accessed 23.03.2015).

McKAY, M. – FANNING, P. (2004) *Poczucie własnej wartości.* Poznań: Dom Wydawniczy REBIS.

MAYOU, R. – BRYANT, B. (1987) *Quality of life after coronary artery surgery.* QJM: An International Journal of Medicine. Vol. 62.

OLEŚ, P. (2002) Jakość życia w zdrowiu i chorobie. In OLEŚ, P. – STEUDEN, S. – TOCZOŁOWSKI, J. (eds.). *Jak świata mniej widzę: zaburzenia widzenia, a jakość życia.* Lublin: Wyd. KUL.

OLEŚ, P. – STEUDEN, S. – TOCZOŁOWSKI, J. (eds.) (2002) *Jak świata mniej widzę: zaburzenia widzenia, a jakość życia.* Lublin: Wyd. KUL.

OSTRZYŻEK, A. (2002) Jakość życia: perspektywa medycyny. In BERNADETTA-KULIK, T. (ed.). *Rehabilitacja. Ostrowiec Świętokrzyski* : Wyd. Stowarzyszenie na Rzecz Rozwoju Wyższej Szkoły Biznezsu i Przedsiębiorczości.

OKŁA W. – STEUDEN, S. (2007) *Jakość życia w chorobie*. Lublin: Wyd. KUL.

PALAK, Z. – LEWICKA, A. – BUJNOWSKA, A. (eds.) (2006) *Jakość życia, a niepełnosprawność*. Lublin: Wyd. UMCS.

PETERMAN, A.H. – CELLA, D. (2000) Quality of Life. In KAZDIN, A. E. (ed). *Encyclopedia of Psychology*. Oxford: Oxford University Press – American Psychological Association. Vol. 6.

ROSTOWSKA, T. (2009) *Małżeństwo, rodzina, praca a jakość życia*. Kraków: Wyd. "Impuls".

UCHNAST, Z. (2007) *Opis wybranych Skal Psychologicznej Jakosci Życia*. Instytut Psychologii KUL, Katedra Psychologii Ogolnej, Lublin (unpublished typescript).

Dziennik Ustaw (Journal of Laws) 2010 no. 228 point 1489 – Rozporządzenie Ministra Edukacji Narodowej z dnia 17 listopada 2010 r. w sprawie warunków organizowania kształcenia, wychowywania i opieki dla dzieci i młodzieży niepełnosprawnych oraz niedostosowanych społecznie w specjalnych przedszkolach, szkołach i oddziałach oraz w ośrodkach (on the conditions for organizing education, upbringing and care for children and youth with disabilities and socially maladjusted in special kindergartens, schools and departments and centres).

7 Quality of Life of Pupils with Hearing Impairment

7.1 Introduction

The idea of integration in view of 80-million disabled Europeans and their dignified life on equal rights as part of the community have been taken into account in the "Europe 2020" Programme for the years 2010 - 2020. The programme contains strategies for social actions for education, fighting poverty and social exclusion, which are aimed at the creation of conditions favouring social inclusion of the disabled and the improvement of their life quality. The awareness of the rights and obligations to make autonomous choices, create one's own social and cultural identity, which are guaranteed by declarations of the nature of European or international law, has led to the situation where modern society is more diversified internally than the older generation. The idea of integration, rooted in the European tradition and understood as unification of people and co-existence of cultures is emphasized and preferred in the interpenetration of the values of a minority and majority, which allow to create social inclusion in terms of equality and reciprocity and not discrimination and marginalization. In the times of liquid modernity we observe the blurring of differences between people, and the opening of frontiers and variety is/becomes normal. Is it always the case? How are inclusion and discrimination, being part of individual man's existence and his/her social space perceived by diversified society in everyday life?

Answers to the questions posed and discussion concerning the life quality of the disabled in the conditions of social inclusion are most frequently elaborated in the scope of possibilities, limits and conditioning of this process of consolidation of educational, professional and social space with reference to children, young adolescents and adults. I will present the approach to the multifaceted issue by reference to theoretical assumptions of inclusive pedagogy as a norm and alternative in educational actions and to examples of social inclusion of progressive and subjective evaluation of life quality of hearing impaired pupils in the conditions of inclusive education.

7.2 Multidimensionality of Inclusion and Quality of Life

I shall start my reflection on the multiplicity of dimensions of the issue of social inclusion of the hearing impaired persons with the following question: Is it possible to mark the limits and scope of inclusion? Is it possible to talk about absolute inclusion? Are diversified social groups divided by a borderline which is set by ourselves?

The opening of frontiers means exceeding certain capacities. Positive experiences of integrated educational system for disabled pupils in Poland are an example of the strategy of promoting social inclusion in inclusive education as an alternative option in educational actions. It has to be noted, however, that free choice of the scope and forms of supporting the development of hearing impaired children cannot be the crossing of limits of their possibilities but an opening. This means opening for the creation of support network in life natural environment that enables the improvement of life quality of diversified persons on the basis of statutorily guaranteed rights and obligations.

The Convention of the Rights of Persons with Disabilities passed by the UNO and ratified by Poland in 2012 recognizes a full autonomy and independence of persons with disabilities, including the freedom of making their own choices. It ensures an inclusive system of education that enables integration at all levels of education and introduction of rational improvements according to individual needs. It enables one to have support within universal education and, in the case of hearing impaired persons, to support their learning by sign language or other alternative methods, means and forms of communication (Dz. U. 25.X.2012, poz. 1169). The Act on sign language and other means supporting communication has also been binding in Poland since 2012 (Dz. U. 19.VIII.20122). The Act regulates the direction of the adopted legal solutions and at the same time is the recommendation for the care, support, education and rehabilitation of the hearing impaired persons.

What is the significance of respecting the quoted legal regulations binding in Poland for the theory and practice of inclusive education? I shall present a number of selected examples of social inclusion, progressive and subjective evaluation of exclusion from the perspective of hearing impaired persons and their parents.

The aim of inclusive education is ensuring the access to education to all children that require individualized support, that is to the healthy or disabled ones, with special/specific educational needs, threatened by disability or exclusion. In Poland, every school is subject to evaluation of the quality of its teaching, and the success of the school is most frequently identified with pupils' good grades and achievements measured in competence tests and successes in competitions. Are formal school achievements of deaf pupils or those with intellectual disability perceived in the categories of success or educational difficulties of the school/class? Gajdzica (2013, p. 54) emphasizes that in our search for the concept of integrated education successes have to be of subjective nature and the achievements of pupils and teachers are not mere didactic successes. They have to be synchronized with educational success which creates "the culture of integrated education" and remains in the sphere of personal feelings of teachers, pupils and their parents.

One of the principles governing the inclusive education is its transdiciplinary nature (Lechta 2010). An implication for the practical implementation of inclusive education is transforming the individual work of the teacher with the child in the work of multi-specialist team along with active cooperation of parents (Podgórska-Jachnik 2011). This requires the discarding of the old model of conduct in the didactic and educational process as well as a change of thinking of homogeneity of educational solutions as a long-term and thoughtful obligation. For the practice of inclusive education this means recognition and application of sign language and bilingualism as alternative forms of communication. Although in the provisions of the Act the obligation to apply the selected method of communication is not defined, but the skill of using sign language should be obligatory not only for special educators, speech therapists but also for the parents and relatives of the deaf child.

There is a risk that focusing on the legal act relieves from ethical responsibility the people who are not defined in the Act (parents, teachers or speech therapists). In addition to this, those people are often responsible for choice of the direction of rehabilitation and education of children/persons with the damaged hearing organ and in that way, they can determine the future life quality of the impaired persons. From my own observations, it appears that communication between the hearing and poorly hearing mothers and their hearing impaired children is perceived as the expectations of the linguistic majority towards the minority. It means that in practice every other mother expects and orders that their hearing-impaired children communicate with sound language, while hearing-impaired mothers prefer bilingualism. Let us not forget that the freedom of choice is an ethical category and perceiving deaf people as "a different" linguistic and cultural minority also arises numerous controversies among parents.

How do students with hearing impairment perceive the problem of autonomy, support and school requirements? How do they perceive relationships, means of communication and satisfaction from education? In recent years, issues like these have been researching in connection to the meaning of quality of life of people with disabilities. The concept of quality of life is a category of multi-dimensionality, which causes some conceptual differences and the lack of unanimity range of meanings (Zabłocki 2013, Zawiślak 2006, Żyta 2006). Frequently the quality of life of people with disabilities is a reflection on the border of humanities, social, medical, but also technical and economic in three dimensions: health, family home, school/work in the context of individual and social (Zablocki 2013). The difficulties of definition make most often refer to indicators that this quality designate areas: emotional state, physical, interpersonal relationships, being personal, material, autonomous decision, integration (Schalockza, Zablocki 2013, Żyta 2006). Therefore, the importance of research on the perception of the psychosocial environment at schools for deaf students is increasing and some findings about the dimension of support, autonomy and requirements are relevant to the teaching theory and practice. Individual and subjective perceived psychosocial school environment is one of the measures of culture, education and inclusive determinant of quality of life.

7.3 Subjective Evaluation of Quality of Life in the Light of Pupils with Hearing Impairment

Education plays a significant role in creating social inclusion. Since the beginning of establishing the educational system, the school's task has been to support the pupils' development by creating optimal conditions for learning. Education cannot just be a simple preparation for adult life, adaptation to the changing conditions, but it should be a promotor and accelerator of desired changes that occur in the modern world. For every person school is an important living space, where we spend about ¼ of the entire day for a dozen or so years of our lives. That is why the studies concerning the perception of psychosocial environment of the school by pupils in the context of support and self-assessment are so important for the educational theory and practice. In Poland, since 1990, they carried out an international research on health and health behaviour of young people (HBSC), but do not participate in them aurally disabled students. Individual and subjective perceived psychosocial school environment is one of the measures of culture, education and inclusive determinant of quality of life.

To illustrate the perception of support in the school environment and self-evaluation of health, I shall refer to my own studies on the subjective image of health and health-promoting behaviours of pupils with hearing defect (Gunia 2010). The study included 142 pupils with hearing defect at junior secondary schools in the system of special needs education and in the system of generally accessible schools. The selection of the group under study was purposeful. It appears from the analysis of statistical data that in recent years the number of hearing impaired pupils learning at generally accessible schools at the primary and junior secondary levels has slightly increased. In the school year 2013/14 2089 pupils attended generally accessible junior secondary schools and 583 attended special education schools.

The purpose of the studies presented has been the determination of the image of psychosocial environment of the school in the opinion of the hearing impaired adolescents between 13 and 17 years of age. On the basis of their replies the attitude of the persons under study to the following was established:

1. pupils' autonomy, taking into account their participation in activities and school life as well as in decision making;
2. support by persons from three closest social groups, that is teachers, peers and parents;
3. requirements related to learning at school.

The method of diagnostic survey was applied with the support of the questionnaire entitled "*Social environment of school as perceived by pupils*". This is a version of the questionnaire (interview) used in international Cross-National Study on Health Behaviour in School-aged Children (HBSC), under the auspices of the World Health Organisation – Regional Office for Europe (Woynarowska, Mazur, 2004, 2012), to determine the subjective assessment of quality of life in three dimensions: autonomy, support, school requirements.

For the needs of this study certain findings from studies have been selected in order to illustrate the issues discussed – subjective assessment of the culture of inclusive education:

• The hearing impaired believe that what determines the autonomy of pupils in the social environment of the school is the opportunity of working at one's own individual pace. All the persons included in the study noted that they could only to a small degree influence the way that time was used in lessons or participate in establishing rules.

- Hearing impaired pupils critically perceive the educational requirements as difficult and exhausting work which is time consuming for them.
- Young people educated at special education schools receive greater support from their teachers and schoolmates than their hearing impaired peers in generally accessible schools (the differences are statistically significant).
- Support given to adolescents by their parents and the evaluation of school requirements is ranked higher (more positively) by hearing impaired pupils in universal/integrated schools than by their hearing impaired peers at special education schools. Those differences prove the statistical significance ($p < 0.05$).

Conclusions: one has to note that perceiving oneself in various social spaces is searching for one's own potential (resources) and a challenge to create a positive value of inclusion, guaranteed by the legislation binding in Poland. Can one therefore determine the limits of social inclusion of disabled persons? The examples given prove that pursuing the univocal image of social inclusion of hearing impaired persons is illusive as the disabled persons just like healthy ones are not a homogenous social group. Bartnikowska (2010) believes that this is a manifestation of autonomous views, subjectively perceived marginalization or inclusion. Some "fully identify with minority linguistic and cultural created by people with impaired hearing," others "integrated environmental hearing does not seek to ensure that represent different culture" (2010, pp. 27 – 41).

7.4 Conclusion

To complete this presentation of the selected issues of a subjective evaluation of the life quality of hearing impaired persons in the context of inclusive education I shall refer to the theory by Antonovsky (1995). In the perspective of the challenges of modern paradigms in educational sciences and in view of the binding legislative solutions, one has to assume that inclusion and marginalization do not exclude one another, but have to be treated as two extremes of a continuum. This is in accordance with the theoretical assumptions of inclusive pedagogy which is "an undertaking for a symbiosis of universal education and special needs education (...) [and] does not mean the liquidation of special needs education" and special needs schools system (Lechta 2010, p. 326). According to the adopted thesis, a hearing impaired person moves in one or another direction throughout their lives, depending on their personal resources and limitations resulting from the disorders of their efficiency, including hearing disorders and in the context of social, cultural, political and economic environment, that is mutual interaction of an individual and the outside world.

Literature

ANTONOVSKY, A. (1995) *Rozwikłanie tajemnicy zdrowia*. Warszawa: Fundacja IPN.

BARTNIKOWSKA, U. (2010) Przemiany w postrzeganiu osób z uszkodzonym słuchem i ich wpływ na obraz współczesnej surdopedagogiki. In PRZYBYLINSKI, S. (ed.). *Pedagogika specjalna – tak wiele pozostaje dla nas tajemnicą...* Olsztyn, Wydawnictwo Uniwersytetu Warmińsko-Mazurskiego.

Dz. U. z dnia 19. VIII. 2011 r.

Dz. U. z dnia 25.X. 2012 r., poz. 1169.

GAJDZICA, Z. (2013) *Kategorie sukcesów w opiniach nauczycieli klas integracyjnych jako przyczynek do poszukiwania koncepcji edukacji integracyjnej*. Kraków: Oficyna Wydawnicza "Impuls".

GUNIA, G. (2010). *Subiektywny obraz zdrowia oraz zachowań zdrowotnych uczniów z wadą słuchu. Prace Monograficzne 553.* Kraków: Wydawnictwo Naukowe Uniwersytetu Pedagogicznego im KEN.

LECHTA, V. (2010). Pedagogika inkluzyjna. In ŚLIWERSKI, B. (ed.). *Pedagogika tom 4.* Sopot : Gdańskie Wydawnictwo Psychologiczne

PODGÓRSKA-JACHNIK, D. (2011) Uwarunkowania. i perspektywy edukacji włączającej osób z uszkodzonym słuchem. In *Edukacja niesłyszących. Publikacja konferencyjna.* http://www.pzg.lodz.pl/attachments/category/66/edukacjanieslyszacych.pdf.

WOYNAROWSKA, B. – MAZUR, J. (2012) *Tendencje zmian zachowań zdrowotnych i wybranych wskaźników zdrowia młodzieży szkolnej w latach 1990-2010*. Warszawa: Instytut Matki i Dziecka, Wydział Pedgogiczny, Uniwersytet Warszawski.

WOYNAROWSKA, B. – MAZUR, J. (eds.) (2004) Postrzeganie środowiska psychospołecznego szkoły przez uczniów w Polsce i innych krajach. Raport z badań. Warszawa: Wydział Pedagogiczny Uniwersytet Warszawski.

ZABŁOCKI, K. J. – WOŹNIAK, W. (2013) Jakość życia osób z niepełnosprawnością. Łódzkie Studia Teologiczne, 22, pp. 223 – 228.

ZAWIŚLAK, A. (2006) Koncepcja jakości życia osób z upośledzeniem umysłowym w niektórych współczesnych ujęciach teoretycznych. In PALAK, Z. – LEWICKA, A. – A. BUJNOWSKA. (eds.). *Jakość życia a niepełnosprawność. Konteksty psychopedagogiczne.* Lublin: Wydawnictwo UMCS.

ŻYTA, A. – NOSARZEWSKA, S. (2006) Jakość życia osób niepełnosprawnych – wielość spojrzeń In PALAK, Z. – LEWICKA, A. – BUJNOWSKA. A. (eds.). *Jakość życia a niepełnosprawność. Konteksty psychopedagogiczne.* Lublin: Wydawnictwo UMCS.

8 Included Pupils with Hearing Impairment

8.1 Introduction

Since 1999, the University of Munich has been running an intensive research program focusing on the inclusion of hearing impaired pre-school and school pupils in mainstream institutions. The research project comprised to date (2016) 19 modules (sub-projects). Within the field of inclusion of children and adolescents with disabilities, it is certainly the most comprehensive and differentiated study in Germany, focusing exclusively on children and adolescents with hearing impairment. Each model took between one and three years.

The individual sub-projects (Table 1) study the integrative/inclusive situation from very different perspectives, e.g. from the pupils' viewpoints, from those of their (hearing) peers, their teachers, the school itself, the specialist HI teachers (inclusion support), their parents and the respective Ministry of Education inspectors. Further studies focus on the didactics and methodology for integrative teaching. Last not least, the research pro-

Tab. 1. Integration/Inclusion of the Hearing Impaired in Mainstream Institutions – Overview of the Munich Research Project

Module	I	II	III	IV	V
Topic	Hearing impaired children and adolescents in mainstream schools	Hearing impaired children and adolescents in mainstream schools	Reasons for transfer from mainstream to special education (SEN) centres	Hearing impaired children in mainstream and inclusive kindergartens	Integrative teaching with hearing impaired pupils
Research subject	Teachers of SEN support for hearing impaired pupils Hearing impaired adults	Teachers at mainstream schools Hearing impaired pupils	Hearing impaired school switchers parents teachers at mainstream schools; teachers at SEN	Hearing impaired children Parents Nursery school teachers speech training/development	Didactics and methodology for integrative teaching
Module	VI	VII	VIII	IX	X
Topic	Expectations and experience of parents of integrated children with HI	Risks in schoolintegration	Risks in preschoolintegration	Cooperation between SEN and mainstream teachers	Social inclusion in the classroom
Research subjects	Parents	Translation of S.I.F.T.E.R. into German HI pupils	Translation of preschool S.I.F.T.E.R. into German HI preschool children	SEN teachers Mainstream school teachers	Hearing impaired pupils hearing peers
Module	XI	XII	XIII	XIV	XV
Topic	Use of audio technical devices	Article 24 of UN Convention on Human Rights	School-related advice from SEN(Mobile support service)	Materials for inclusive teaching	Hearing impaired youths in dual vocational training
Research subject	Participation in integrative teaching	Ministry of Education inspectors	HI pupils	Practice/school	Hearing impairedtrainees
Module	XVI	XVII	XVIII	XIX	
Topic	Deaf children with sign teachers at mainstream schools	Hearing impaired pupils at secondary schools	Included HI children and adolescents outside school	Quality offensive of teacher training	
Research subject	Deaf children with GSAcompetence in the inclusive situation	Secondary school pupils	Pupils at secondary school age (social situation, puberty, networks)	Co-learning situation between normal hearing peers and HI pupils	

gram reports on the availability of the audio and visual components necessary for successful classroom and social communication for HI pupils. An internal or external paid member of staff supports each sub-project.

The UN Convention on Human Rights for the Disabled – in particular the Education Article 24 – implemented in Germany in 2009, added impetus to the discussion on mainstream education for all children and adolescents, with or without handicap.

Selected empirical findings of Module I, III, VI and X are presented below. These were selected for their empirical approach towards social relationships between pupils with and without hearing impairment. Essentially, the information reports on "integration". Inclusion is to be seen as a prospective target rather than a reality. Now, we were "on the way" to inclusion. In practice, it is the task of schools to set up the necessary conditions and organisational measures paramount to a successful implementation of inclusion.

Apart from Module XII, which is not included in the findings below, due to economic factors governing time and funding all surveys included in the research program were confined to Bavaria.

8.2 Social Integration

Within the framework of research activities to date, the Module X subproject is the one, which most directly and comprehensively focuses on the social integration of children and adolescents with hearing impairment. Under the heading 'Gräfen 2015', it is presented as the first in the selected findings below.

Within the framework of the sub-project, two scientific issues were considered:

1. How are social relationships between classmates set up during school and leisure?
2. How do pupils with hearing impairment fare emotionally?
   (Gräfen 2015, 70).

Answers were collated in the form of a questionnaire, comprising sociometric data, the status of the HI pupil in class and the class situation. In content and structure, it followed the same format as

- The findings of preceding projects (Module I – IX)
- The Wauters/Knoors (2008) Netherland study and

- 2003 Rauer/Schuck (FEESS 3-4) questionnaires recording the emotional and social experiences of primary school children attending the third and fourth grades.

Additional interviews with the HI pupils were conducted. These focused on social relationships at school and leisure, including self-evaluation of the social situation.

The investigation included 16 school classes, each with one to three HI pupils from the 2nd to the 10th grades. This yielded a total of 334 pupils with normal hearing and 21 pupils with all types of (peripheral) hearing impairment. The degree of hearing impairment ranged from mild to profound. The pupils participating in the survey represented all types of schools as follows: 22.25% Primary School (in Bavaria grades 1 – 4), 25.92% Middle School, 11.27% *Realschule* (Secondary School) and 40.56 % Grammar School.

To establish the social status of HI pupils in class and their relationships with class peers, (*research question* 1), socio-metric data was included in the questionnaire. For this purpose, the 15 socio-metric elements of the Wauters/Knoors (2008) study were used. These focus on popularity, rejection, helpfulness, the victim of bullying, the troublemaker, the spiteful, the friendly, the nuisance, the cooperative, the uncooperative, the ones invited/not invited to birthdays as well as the inclusion status during school breaks. The desired information was elicited with questions such as: "Which of your classmates do you like best?" (Popularity), or "Which of your classmates do you like the least?" (Rejection), or "Which of your classmates are often made fun of or bullied?" or "Which classmate do you go to when you need help?"

Individual analysis of the participating classes revealed that HI pupils assume a very different status in each class and the social situation of the individual pupil varies considerably, ranging from good to extremely negative social communication both inside and outside the classroom. This is apparent in both the self-evaluated and external assessments. Another feature is that there is greater heterogeneity in the HI pupil sector. This defies all binding or definitive statements. Instead, one resorts to the term 'tendencies'. Noticeable, however, is the fact that HI pupils have a lower rating by their classmates than their hearing peers do. They hold an inferior position in class and they tend to play a negative role. On average, in all positive criteria, (e.g. popularity, helpfulness, friendships, team working, inclusion in birthday invitations/ during intervals) the HI pupils received fewer mentions than their hearing classmates do. In the negative criteria (bullying, quarrelling, disturbance, being a nuisance, uncooperativeness, exclusion from invitations) the HI pupils likewise came off worse than their classmates (Gräfen 2015, 538f.).

Further conclusions governing social and emotional integration were drawn from interviews held with the HI pupils. The majority of HI pupils feel they are well integrated but nevertheless report on a vast number of problems affecting their daily lives. These are largely to do with their peer relationships during leisure time activities, with incidents of wrangling or exclusion, as well as the perceived inequality of classroom status (Gräfen 2015, 540).

Responses to the *second round of questioning* include the self-assessment of HI pupils as regards "social integration", "class atmosphere" and "scholarly self-perception":

- On the subject of "social integration", HI pupils rate their integration better than their hearing pupils do.
- On average, classroom atmosphere is rated equally by hearing and HI pupils.
- In the case of "scholarly perception", HI pupils rate themselves higher than a great number of hearing peers.
  (cf. Gräfen 2015, 541f.).

According to Gräfen (2015, 542), there are two possible explanations for this last phenomenon: it is possible that HI pupils actually do perform well in their schoolwork, otherwise they would suffer in the integrative situation. A further possibility is that HI pupils perceive themselves as superior scholars compared with their hearing peers in that being handicapped; they need to put more time and effort into their schoolwork to achieve the same results as their hearing classmates.

A *thorough* examination of the interview responses highlights the problems experienced by the HI pupils in class, affecting their relationships with hearing peers as well as their emotional well-being in general.

A comparison of the findings spanning the overall school period highlights the fact that as pupils move up the school, there is an increasing decline in integration and general contentment at school. This, however, is true for both hearing and HI pupils alike.

One of the problem areas is the social situation during school intervals, although HI and hearing pupils are affected alike. This is confirmed not only in the Gräfen study (2015), but also in the Audeoud/Wertli (2011) study.

On the surface, it would appear that HI and hearing peer pupils are treated as equals: popular pupils and less popular (rejected/bullied) ones exist everywhere. In terms of popularity, the majority of HI pupils score an average rating.

In the interview, six of the 21 HI pupils admitted to having problems with their classmates, which they attributed to their hearing impairment (e.g. bullying to do with their hearing devices).

HI pupils came off worse in the survey question "Which classmate do you like the best?" They are frequently bullied, less frequently invited to birthday parties and frequently rejected by their classmates. Furthermore, they are seldom mentioned as friends, less frequently chosen as a team-worker, less frequently invited home and less frequently sought after during the school interval.

8.3 Social and Emotional Well-Being of Pupils with Hearing Impairment

Conclusions governing social and emotional well-being can be drawn from the sub-project entitled "Hearing Impaired Pupils in Mainstream Education" (Schmitt 2003). In this research program, 216 integrated HI pupils attending grades 3 to 7 were studied using the Haeberlin et al. (1998) questionnaire. This comprises 15 questions on performance-related integration (self-assessment of classroom ability), social integration (own assessment of relationships with fellow pupils) and emotional integration (self-assessment). These were supplemented by 15 questions directly related to hearing impairment.

The findings on social and emotional integration relevant to the discussion are presented in the table below.

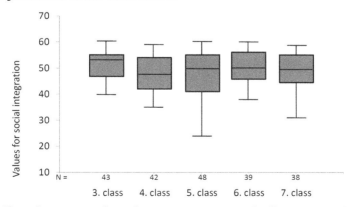

Fig. 1. Comparison of social integration in 3 – 7 grades (Lönne 2009, 28)

As may be deduced from diagram 1, social integration throughout grades 3-7 is relatively stable. In the 5ᵗʰ grade, there is evidence of a greater dispersion than in other school years. Otherwise, there is no significant variance between the school years. Lönne (2009, 29) confirms that the same picture emerges in the comparison of types of school.

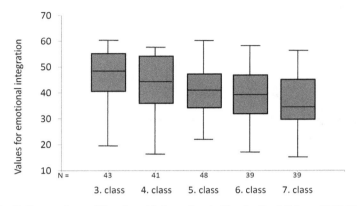

Fig. 2. Comparison of Emotional Integration in Grades 3 – 7 (Lönne 2009, 31)

Figure 2 shows a clearly recognisable decline in emotional integration, becoming progressively lower as pupils progress through school. There is a significant drop in mean values. Emotional well-being becomes increasingly negative, with isolated responses reaching the absolute minimal values in the 4ᵗʰ and 7ᵗʰ grades. Many HI pupils place a cross at the most negative criteria for every question relating to emotional integration (Lönne 2009, 30). Reasons for this may only be assumed: in Bavaria selection entry to the various secondary schools – Middle/Realschule or Grammar school- takes place at the end of the 4ᵗʰ grade. Increased competition poses a burden on the pupil. The 7ᵗʰ year is considered to be the mid-pubertal phase. For integration, the period of puberty is recognised as the most difficult time of all.

8.4 Expectations and Experience of the Parents

Parents play an important role in the integration and inclusion process. One of the findings in the research program reveals that the degree of integration and inclusion is largely influenced by the parents, in that they are constantly at the side of their HI child, e.g. in helping with pre-school or after-school learning or help with homework. In sub-project VI "Expectations and Experience of Parents of Integrated School Children", 452 parents of integrated HI pupils were included in a questionnaire. (Leonhardt/ Ludwig 2007; Ludwig 2009). The participants included parents of children with moderate to profound hearing impairment from every type of school: 38 % at primary school, 16 % at middle school, 21 % at Realschule und 25 % at grammar school.

A third of the parents (33 %) claimed there were social difficulties between their child and fellow classmates. The frequency of these problems was predominantly assessed as "occasional" (35 %) and "seldom" (Ludwig 2009, 167). 18 parents reported that their hearing impaired child had no school friends. One may assume that this is due to the hearing impairment.

The social problems of their children prove burdensome to the parents (fig. 3). Most parents feel "moderately stressed". The stress factor is probably stronger (19 %) (cf. Ludwig 2009, 168).

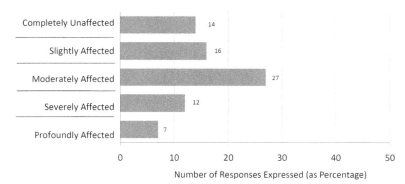

Fig. 3. Stress Level of Parents Affected by the Social Relationships of their Child with Fellow Classmates (n=179; no response: 43, representing 24 % of the study participants) (Ludwig 2009, 167).

8.5 Reasons for Transfer from Mainstream to SEN Facilities

Assumptions governing the social situation of the integrated school-child with hearing impairment can also be made from the information outlined in sub-project III, which focuses on the reasons for and consequences of changing from mainstream schools to SEN facilities. In this study, 12 HI pupils transferring from mainstream schools to SEN institutions (Förder-zentrum, Förderschwerpunkt Hören) were interviewed together with their parents, mainstream teachers and subsequent SEN teachers, representing a total of 48 interviews (Lindner 2007).

The negative experience of HI pupils transferring from mainstream schools to SEN schools was mainly due to bullying. Bullying is understood as repeated and systematic aggression towards the weaker, over a certain period (cf. Hanewinkel/Knaack 1979). In this context of bullying, one distinguishes between physical bullying (e.g. pushing, kicking, mugging), or verbal bullying (e.g. offensive language or derision) and indirect bullying (e.g. ignoring or snubbing).

HI pupils mostly perceived bullying in the verbal form, such as poking fun at their hearing disability or consequences thereof (irregular pronunciation, repeated questions, inability to comprehend or the hearing aids they wore). In extreme cases, HI pupils develop psychosomatic disorders. In addition, conscious snubbing of HI pupils has a disturbing effect on these pupils. As in the later modules, Module X likewise reveals that they are seldom invited to birthday parties or included in school interval activities. This is distressing for children and adolescents alike. It should be pointed out, however, that not all bullying perceived as such by HI pupils is in fact bullying. The interviews conducted clearly reveal that even pushing or moving a chair is perceived as a personal attack, since this affects their hearing and speech comprehension. The mental stress posed by hearing impairment would appear to influence mental perception (Lindner 2009, 196).

The HI pupils are sometimes caught up in a vicious circle. Some of the victims, as already mentioned, are teased because of their hearing devices and they stop wearing them as a result. This, in turn, affects their comprehension ability in both the classroom and the schoolyard, alienating them

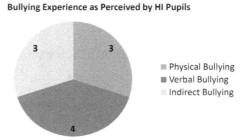

Fig. 4. Bullying as experienced by HI pupils in mainstream schools (Lindner 2009, 195)

even further. Lindner (2009, 196) confirms that such situations are likely to occur in the absence of a visiting SEN specialist.

Interviews with the parents of HI pupils confirm these statements. They also highlight the fact that their children are victims of verbal bullying. Due to restricted speech comprehension, HI children and adolescents are often subjected to misunderstanding, which they perceive as bullying. Some parents point out that their children, unable to assert themselves, react sensitively towards their classmates.

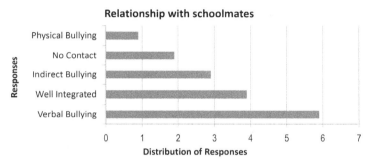

Fig. 5. Bullying experienceas perceived by parents of HI children in mainstream schools (Lindner 2009, 19)

8.6 Conclusion

Although the social aspect is highlighted as an important factor in the success of school integration by HI specialists and the Hearing Impaired alike, it can be seen that on a daily basis, social "equality" or acceptance of HI pupils is not yet firmly rooted. Organised, or desired school integration does not necessarily imply a positive outcome for social integration.

Hearing schoolchildren are not fully aware of the problems of hearing impairment their HI classmates have to cope with – such as delayed auditory register, inadequate speech understanding and restricted communication. Without this knowledge or understanding, hearing children are unable to react sensitively towards their HI classmates.

It should also be noted that "school inclusion" is anticipated very differently by parents of handicapped children, according to the type of handicap. Parents of mentally handicapped children are e.g. primarily concerned that their son or daughter will be accepted socially. Parents of hearing impaired children, on the other hand, expect not only social acceptance but also a good educational qualification for their child. As with social integration, such expectations usually become apparent during the integration process (and increasingly during the inclusion process).

There is an increasing tendency for parents of hearing impaired children to opt for school integration, not only to avoid long journeys to special schools or weekly boarding schools or to preserve the contact with children in the neighbourhood, but also because they are influenced by the political trends towards this type of education.

Over the years, numerous projects on the subject of school inclusion have evolved. The focus of these studies varies considerably. With a view to social relationships, there is a need for more research, not only focusing on the classroom or school but also on social relationship settings for leisure time. For the psychological well-being of the integrated/included pupil, contact with other HI pupils is also important. Being with peers in the same situation seems to relieve the mental burden.

Literature

AUDEOUD, M. – WERTLI, E. (2010) *Alltagserleben hörgeschädigter Menschen.* Perspektiven Schweizerischer Hörgeschädigtenforschung. In Schweizerische Zeitschrift für Heilpädagogik, 15, pp. 44 – 49.

GRÄFEN, C. (2015) *Die soziale Situation integriert beschulter Kinder und Jugendlicher mit Hörschädigung an der allgemeinen Schule.* Kovač, Hamburg.

HAEBERLIN, U. – MOSER, U. – BLESS, G. – KLAGHOFER, R. (1989) *Integration in die Schulklasse. Fragebogen zur Erfassung von Dimensionen der Integration von Schülern FDI 4-6.* Bern/Stuttgart: Haupt.

HANEWINKEL, R. – KNAACK, R. (1997) *Mobbing: Eine Fragebogenstudie zum Ausmaß von Aggression und Gewalt an Schulen.* In Empirische Pädagogik. Zeitschrift zu Theorie und Praxis erziehungswissenschaftlicher Forschung, 11, 3, pp. 403 – 422.

LEONHARDT, A. (ed.) (2009) *Hörgeschädigte Schüler in der allgemeinen Schule. Theorie und Praxis der Integration.* Stuttgart: Kohlhammer.

LEONHARDT, A. – LUDWIG, K. (2007) *"Es ist ein unwahrscheinlicher Kraftakt...". Elternerfahrungen zur schulischen Integration.* In Schnecke, 18, 55, pp. 29 – 32.

LINDNER, B. (2007) *Schulische Integration Hörgeschädigter in Bayern: Untersuchung zu den Ursachen und Folgen des Wechsels von der allgemeinen Schule an das Förderzentrum, Förderschwerpunkt Hören.* Dissertation, LMU München: Fakultät für Psychologie und Pädagogik. https://edoc.ub.uni-muenchen.de/7941/.

LINDNER, B. (2009) „Soviel Integration wie möglich – so viele Sondereinrichtungen wie nötig."Warum wechseln hörgeschädigte Schüler von der allgemeinen Schule an Förderzentren, Förderschwerpunkt Hören? In LEONHARDT, A. (ed.). Hörgeschädigte Schüler in der allgemeinen Schule. Theorie und Praxis der Integration. Stuttgart: Kohlhammer, pp. 180 – 217.

LÖNNE, J. (2009) Einschätzung der Integrationssituation durch die hörgeschädigten Schüler. In LEONHARDT, A. (ed.). Hörgeschädigte Schüler in der allgemeinen Schule. Theorie und Praxis der Integration. Stuttgart: Kohlhammer, pp. 23 – 39.

LUDWIG, K. (2009) Eltern und Integration – Erfahrungen und Erwartungen. In LEONHARDT, A. (ed.). Hörgeschädigte Schüler in der allgemeinen Schule. Theorie und Praxis der Integration. Stuttgart: Kohlhammer, pp. 148 – 179.

RAUER, W. – SCHUCK, K.-D. (2003) Fragebogen zur Erfassung emotionaler und sozialer Schulerfahrungen von Grundschulkindern dritter und vierter Klassen (FEESS 3-4). Göttingen.

SCHMITT, J. (2003) Hörgeschädigte Kinder und Jugendliche in allgemeinen Schulen. Untersuchung von schulischer Einzelintegration in Bayern unter besonderer Berücksichtigung des Übergangs in die Sekundarstufe.Aachen: Shaker.

WAUTERS, L. – KNOORS, H. (2008) Social Integration of Deaf Children in Inclusive Settings. In Journal of Deaf Studies and Deaf Education, 13, pp. 21 – 36.

LINDNER, B. (2009) „Soviel Integration wie möglich – so viele Sondereinrichtungen wie nötig."Warum wechseln hörgeschädigte Schüler von der allgemeinen Schule an Förderzentren, Förderschwerpunkt Hören? In LEONHARDT, A. (ed.). Hörgeschädigte Schüler in der allgemeinen Schule. Theorie und Praxis der Integration. Stuttgart: Kohlhammer, pp. 180 – 217.

LÖNNE, J. (2009) Einschätzung der Integrationssituation durch die hörgeschädigten Schüler. In LEONHARDT, A. (ed.). Hörgeschädigte Schüler in der allgemeinen Schule. Theorie und Praxis der Integration. Stuttgart: Kohlhammer, pp. 23 – 39.

LUDWIG, K. (2009) Eltern und Integration – Erfahrungen und Erwartungen. In LEONHARDT, A. (ed.). Hörgeschädigte Schüler in der allgemeinen Schule. Theorie und Praxis der Integration. Stuttgart: Kohlhammer, pp. 148 – 179.

RAUER, W. – SCHUCK, K.-D. (2003) Fragebogen zur Erfassung emotionaler und sozialer Schulerfahrungen von Grundschulkindern dritter und vierter Klassen (FEESS 3-4). Göttingen.

SCHMITT, J. (2003) Hörgeschädigte Kinder und Jugendliche in allgemeinen Schulen. Untersuchung von schulischer Einzelintegration in Bayern unter besonderer Berücksichtigung des Übergangs in die Sekundarstufe.Aachen: Shaker.

WAUTERS, L. – KNOORS, H. (2008) Social Integration of Deaf Children in Inclusive Settings. In Journal of Deaf Studies and Deaf Education, 13, pp. 21 – 36.

9 The Influence of UN Convention

9.1 Introduction

According to the national survey in Hungary in 2011, the number of persons with hearing impairment is 71585, 8571 of whom are deaf.

The number of hearing impaired students attending special institutions of the hearing impaired is 334, and the number of those who are in integrated settings are 1483.

In Hungary, there has been compulsory schooling for the public since 1770, and it has also been extended to pupils with special educational needs since the 19th century. Consequently, a widespread and well-differentiated special institutional system exists in today's Hungary. Besides, it is important to mention that this process of institutional development concerning special education has not finished yet. For example, we can also see the establishment of special classes for pupils with autism or speech impairment.

In Hungary 8 special schools have been established for hearing impaired pupils, with additional dormitory facilities. The first special boarding school for them was established more than 200 years ago. One of these institutions provides teaching only for hard of hearing pupils, and the others cater for both deaf and hard of hearing students.

These schools provide services from early intervention to vocational training program all over the country.

The educational opportunities of children with hearing impairment are influenced by, among others, the time of occurrence and diagnosis of the hearing impairment and the subsequent services (provision of optimal hearing aid, early intervention, etc.), as well as any additional difficulties accompanying the hearing impairment. Another important factor determining the level of speech acquisition and the selected communication strategies is whether the child comes from a hearing and speaking environment, or a family preferring sign language. In addition to the above-listed factors, the best form of formal education for a child with hearing impairment will also depend on the individual characteristics (e.g. intellectual abilities, verbal proficiency, verbal learning ability and motivation) and the parents' intentions.

The majority of hearing impaired pupils attended these institutions until the 1990s. Since 1993, when the Educational Act was passed, the integration of pupils with special educational needs has been a legal opportunity, and the proportion of hearing impaired students educated in mainstream institutions has been increasing more and more. There are several reasons for this situation: on the one hand, the gradual acceptance of the approaches of inclusion, the continuous decrease of the school-age population, and the policies and regulations of the governments, which supported integration. Strong pressure has been experienced on the part of parents of children with SEN too so that their children get education in the local mainstream school.

Today almost 70 % of these students attend mainstream institutions. The parents have the right to choose the educational environment for their hearing-impaired children. The increasing of the number of integrated pupils is due to technical development of hearing aids, cochlear implantation, UNHS, and early intervention programs. Mainstream schools certainly impose higher requirements on children with hearing impairment, but also equip them better for choosing a career and integration in society.

At the same time, we can observe a change in the population of hearing impaired children attending special schools. The number of pupils in special education has decreased, their needs are more complex in addition to hearing impairment language, learning and social disadvantages can be experienced.

Special institutions use an oral-auditive approach with special emphasis on developing hearing, initiating speech, focus on developing verbal communication and helping speech acquisition at the highest level possible. This approach was reinforced by Gusztáv Bárczi's work, which focused on mobilizing residual hearing before World War II., and by the appearance of hearing aids in the '50s.

9.2 Complex Assessment and Early Intervention Program

In children with multiple difficulties, the development of speech may be rendered more difficult by the other problems accompanying the hearing impairment. In their case, a combination of special methods, including communication in sign language and working individually or in small groups, may be effective.

In Hungary, the National Expert and Rehabilitation Committee for Hearing Assessment recommends a specific school or nursery school for the child on the basis of a complex assessment including medical, psychological and special educational aspects, and the expert opinion on the results of that assessment is a necessary condition for using the free services available for children with hearing impairment.

In Hungary, we have a free early intervention program for every hearing-impaired child immediately after the diagnosis, which is provided mainly in the child's home, or in Special Educational Methodology Centers. In western countries, they are called special educational centres or resource centres and in contrast with the Hungarian situation, they are independent of the special institutions. The changing the role of the special institutions took place at the turn of the 20th – 21st centuries. The institutions of well-known historical background have lost more than half of their students in the past two decades. By the increasing rate of integrated education, it became clear that it was of utmost importance to provide a wide range of services for the pupils with SEN at local schools, which resulted in the dissemination of knowledge accumulated in special institutions. One important characteristic feature of them is that they provide exclusively special educational services. (Csányi 1990; Papp 1995, 2004; Gerebenné 1996; Mesterházi 1998). In the Hungarian system, however, from the 70's in the framework of special institutions for children with hearing and physical impairment the initial types of services were formed, and that was the first step of the establishment of the service system, from which there developed today's Unified Special Educational Methodology Centres (Kőpatakiné, 2004, 2006, 2009; Faragóne, Papp, 2011). Earlier, these centres only had special institutional profile, but nowadays they provide both special educational and integrational services. The Unified Special Educational Methodology Centres with a wide range of services aim at helping the mainstream schools to integrate pupils with SEN how to handle their special needs. On the one hand, the primary target group of their services are the pupils with SEN (specific development, individual or group therapies, Individualised Education Plan (IEP), equipment rental). On the other hand, they also support the mainstream teachers and communities (to form inclusive attitudes, special methodologies, technics, differentiation, retraining, etc.) The cooperation with mainstream institutions and teachers created an absolutely new learning situation, which meant challenge for the special teachers of the Unified Special Educational Methodology Centres, and not only was this cooperation a burden for them, but also meant their change at working conditions (Mile, Papp, 2012).

Since the auditory-verbal method has been the accepted practice in Hungary until now, the target of early interventional program is developing hearing and teaching normal speech. The basis of the early interventional program is the early and exact identification of hearing loss during the neonatal period (Keresztessy, 2012; Baranyi, Fejes 2012). Since 2015, the *Universal Newborn Hearing Screening* program has been compulsory in Hungary with objective and subjective methods. The hearing screening process focuses on risk children, whose check-up is repeated. We have to minimize the problems of hearing testing process, because many children disappear from the system after clinical treatment, and there is inaccurate audiological diagnosis in some cases.

9.3 Formal Education

Deaf children in special schools have 10 years to complete the foundation stage (i.e. years 1 to 8) of education, as their training begins with two preparatory years dedicated to intensive verbal skills development. Children with a partial hearing loss have only one year of preparation. After the completion of primary school, children with hearing impairment may continue their education either in years 9 and 10 of a special school (participating in vocational or special vocational programmes), or in a mainstream secondary school, together with hearing students. Those children whose hearing impairment is coupled with learning difficulties or mental problems can only continue their education in special vocational schools. Compared to other types of secondary schools, vocational schools (and obviously special vocational schools) tend to show much more willingness to take on students with special educational needs, because these schools are already used to a higher diversity among their students, and many of them do not refuse to admit even the most problematic students. In addition to the selected school type, another important issue is the reason for choosing vocational training. As in the case of the students of schools providing vocational training, the reasons behind the choice of vocational training often include poor academic results, which is a factor limiting the choice, and the limited offer of the local school.

From kindergarten age to the end of secondary education the integrated hearing impaired students get extra help from peripatetic teachers in mainstream environment. The form of this extra help can be individual sessions or support in the classroom. Both types of help have different objectives.

While individual sessions aim at coping with special difficulties coming from hearing impairment (e.g. hearing development, literacy, vocabulary, articulation, etc.), the task of the support in the classroom are the following (Mather et al., 2013):

- Optimizing the Listening environment – "deaf-friendly" as possible
- Tips for teachers – introduce the topic before launching into it; do not face the whiteboard; use short sentences etc.
- Using technology – FM system
- Note taking, handouts, etc.
- Visual support
- Tutoring
- Difficulties: language gap, literacy

Hearing impaired student are entitled for some possibilities and facilities, so that their right for equal access to the education should be ensured.

- institutions taking on students with hearing impairment become eligible for extra financial resources for such children;
- one student with hearing impairment can be taken into account as two or three students for the purpose of determining the group/class size;
- free services are made available for the student in accordance with the expert opinion (so-called habilitation/rehabilitation training, speech therapy);
- employment of a special teacher holding a qualification in the required special field (so-called peripatetic special teacher);
- use of special requirements on the schooling of students with special educational needs;
- possibility of exemption from the learning or assessment of certain subjects or parts of the curriculum;
- opportunity of using aids, e.g. for tests and examinations;
- opportunity to choose the form of assessment (e.g. students with hearing impairment may choose to participate in a written examination instead of an oral examination, or in an oral examination instead of a written examination). We might think that students with hearing impairment favour the written form of examination, but surprisingly, there are students with hearing impairment who prefer to take an oral examination instead of a written one.

While the law allows such modification in Hungary, its application is not recommended, unless the need for ensuring equal opportunities so demands. The special needs of students with hearing impairment can justify the following modifications of requirements:

- Extending the training period. This includes the extension of the period of compulsory school attendance, which may be necessary for the acquisition of specific skills or because of the special needs arising from the disability of the individual with the hearing impairment concerned. In the case of mainstream students, the compulsory school age is between 6 and 16, but as far as students with special needs are concerned, this can be extended until age 23.

- Replacing a compulsory subject by another subject. In the case of students with hearing impairment, this may occur in the learning of foreign languages, but students may also be exempted from other subjects in the field of communication or music. In the event of such exemption, the student concerned must learn another subject or participate in habilitation/rehabilitation sessions instead of the lessons from which exemption is granted. Another form of exemption is the possibility that the head of the school only grants exemption from evaluation and assessment, and not from participation, based on the opinion of the experts' committee. In such a case, the student must participate in the lessons, but his or her performance is not evaluated.

Without a formal commitment to inclusion, the success of the inclusion of students with hearing impairment may largely depend on the individual attitude, qualification and commitment of teachers.

What is the next step?

According to overview of the Hungarian situation, we can define some objectives to be achieved both in special education and in integrated setting of students with hearing impairment. Owing to the heterogeneity of student needs in special classes, we have to increase the role of individual sessions. This could enhance feasibility concerning students´ achievement. Regarding students with hearing impairment and some additional disorders, it is essential that alternative ways of communication (augmentative communication, sign language, etc.) were found. It can be a good solution to organize linguistic groups instead of age groups. The chances are that bilingual education that will be introduced in the future could colour the everyday practice of special schools.

What concerns mainstream classes, in which hearing-impaired students are integrated, we would like to increase the proportion of team – teaching, common planning and evaluation with mainstream teachers. We believe that adapting the mainstream class-teaching environment and curriculum to the different needs of students with SEN is at least as effective as individual sessions with children. In the field of integration of students with hearing impairment, it is also important to extend the services to secondary and higher education.

In the past decades, sign language or bilingual methods have not been used officially in the special institutions of the hearing impaired. However, due to the changes of the population teachers have been using sign language more and more, mostly as a complementary way to understand each other better. They have been using signed Hungarian instead of Hungarian Sign Language.

9.4 Habilitation and Rehabilitation Services for Deaf Community

The UN Convention on the Right of Persons with Disabilities and its optional minutes were ratified in Hungary in 2007. The Convention lists the most important rights of persons with disabilities, mainly thinking of hearing impaired people, such as the right of the free use of sign language (21 article), the right for education in sign language (24th article), and the right to maintain the Deaf culture (4th article). As a result of the Convention, the law (number 125) about the Hungarian Sign language and its Use was passed in 2009, in addition to which some other measures were taken. This law, which, secondly after Finland in the European Union, recognises the Deaf community as a linguistic minority, is a complex one, because it applies not only to Hearing-impaired persons, but also to Deaf and Blind people. The Deaf Community have welcomed this approach reflected in the Law, as a consequence of which not only are Hearing impaired people looked upon as handicapped people, but also as members of a linguistic minority. After the enactment of the law, the Hungarian Sign language will be part of the Curriculum as an obligatory subject in special schools, and as an optional subject in integrated settings, and besides the auditory-verbal, auditory-oral methods the choice of bilingual method should also be assured in special schools from the same time. The decision, which method is to be used with the particular child, should be made by the parents.

What is the situation as regards the conditions necessary to realise these changes by the date required by the Law?

The Hungarian Sign Language is an officially recognised but not accredited language, so it is not possible to take a language exam in it. This is an obvious disadvantage as far as hearing people are concerned, because for example they do not get extra points to go to university. Also, this can be a drawback among hearing classmates, who are not interested in learning it. We have trainings for Sign language interpreters, but it means only a secondary certificate, in contrast with other language interpreters, who get a master's degree. We do not have teachers majoring in Sign Language, what is more there is no possibility for anyone to learn it at university. The training of qualified mainstream and special teachers needed for the bilingual programs have not even begun so far. In the past decades sign language or bilingual methods have not been used officially in the special institutions of the hearing impaired. Teachers in the special schools of the Deaf are using sign language due to the changes of the population more and more, mostly as a complementary way of communication.

However, pupils both in special and integrated settings get regular extra help from peripatetic teachers, which is free for the parents. This job is done by special teachers, who are trained at the Barczi Faculty of Special Education to cater for hearing impaired people for four years. They are well-prepared to work in early intervention programs, in special schools, integrated settings and with adult persons. At the same time the training program favours the auditive – oral approach. Students can only choose sign language as an optional course, and the program does not prepare them how to teach in a bilingual classroom.

As far as the 26th article of the UN Convention about habilitation and rehabilitation is concerned, its most important elements are the following:
- services from the earliest ages,
- supporting the participation in their own communities,
- inclusion in the local communities, including access to professionals and helping technologies.

9.5 Conclusion

What is the current situation in Hungary?

Since the auditory-verbal method has been the accepted practice in Hungary up till now, the target of early interventional program is teaching normal speech. There has not existed any early interventional program based on sign language so far, and the conditions in connection with the necessary human resources have not been clarified yet. In international practice Deaf model people help families in the early intervention programs.

There arises an interesting question: does inclusion in local communities work? In the case of integrated hearing impaired pupils, the inclusion in the local communities and among peers has been realised, but they have little or no contact with the Deaf community. On the grounds of our experience it seems that since the 90 % of hearing impaired children are born in hearing families, they do not need this regular contact with the Deaf community in the framework they are accustomed to. At the same time the pupils in special schools have contact with other hearing impaired people and the Deaf community, while their contact with the local communities and hearing peers is poorer. It can lead to further problems that at the end of schooling these students return to their homes, where they have no social contacts except for their family.

Among the habilitation and rehabilitation services for hearing impaired persons, it is important to mention sign language interpreters, who are provided on county level, and the clients are entitled for it free, which means 120 hours per persons per year. In the case of students studying in secondary and higher education, they are entitled for further 120 hours per academic year. As for public services the deaf client does not pay for the sign language interpretation, it is financed by the office itself. At the same time the number of hours of translation is not sufficient.

However, it is essential to put emphasis on the fact that there are no sources from the state for the rehabilitation for example to improve hearing or lip reading skills of adult hearing impaired persons, or those who lose their hearing later in their life. With reference to UN Convention, so as to realise the necessary conditions of rehabilitation further steps and measures should be taken.

In terms of the level of legislation and realisation in practice there is a huge difference in Hungary as far as UN Convention requirements are concerned. Some of them require further financial sources, but it is obvious that a change of attitude is necessary. The chance of the introduction is weakened by the fact that there is no understanding between parents, professionals and members of the Deaf Community which type of bilingual method to choose.

The following changes are advisable to establish the requirements of the Law:
- A decision should be made what bilingual method to introduce.
- Parents should be informed objectively about the two approaches to facilitate their decision-making.
- Teacher training program should be extended with compulsory courses, e.g. HSL, Deaf culture and Community, Methodology of Bilingual education.
- Practising (special) teachers should be retrained for bilingual education.

- Co-operation with Deaf Community is necessary according to the principle "Nothing about Us, without Us".
- The number of Deaf role models and teachers should increase in special education.
- Early intervention program based on bilingualism should be introduced.
- Teachers majoring in Sign Language should be trained.
- A collection of study materials should be compiled.

The commitment of ever present governments in power and cooperation of those participating in the execution process are needed so that Hungary can meet the requirements of the UN Convention in the future.

Literature

Convention on the Right of Persons with Disabilities http://www.un.org/disabilities/default.asp?navid=14&pid=150.

CXXV. Law about the Hungarian Sign language and its Use (2009) www.fogyatekosugy.hu/main.php?folderID=1476.

GROSJEAN, F.: The right of the deaf child to grow up bilingual http://www.francoisgrosjean.ch/the_right_en.html.

JOHNSTONE, D. (1999) The role of resources centers in establishing inclusive education In MARSCHARK, M. et al. (2009) Evidence of best practice models and outcomes in the education of deaf and hard-of hearing children: an international review; NCSE research reports.

MATHER, J. – HARBOR, D. – KNOWELS, A. (2013) Teenagers with Cochlear Implants, The Ear Foundation.

McPHERSON, E. (2011) Moving From Separate, to Equal, to Equitable Schooling: Revisiting School Desegregation Policies. Urban Education. 46(3), pp. 465 – 483.

MILE A. – PAPP G. (2012) Special school, Unified Special Educational Methodology Centres, reference institution In. Iskolakultúra 5. pp. 76 – 83.

MOELLER,P. M ET AL.(2013) Best Practices in Family-Centered Early Intervention for Children Who are Deaf or Hard of Hearing: An International Consensus Statement, Journal of Deaf Studies and Deaf Education 18:4 October 2013, pp. 430 – 445. Downloaded from http://jdsde.oxfordjournals.org/ by guest on 14 October 2013.

PAPP G. – PERLUSZ A. (2012) „...It is essential to pay attention to the process and react to them. In ZÁSZKALICZKY P. (ed.). Conditions and limits of social and school integration. Eötvös Loránd University Bárczi Gusztáv Faculty of Special Education Budapest, pp. 179 – 200.

PERLUSZ, A. – STEFANIK, K. – ZÁSZKALICZKY, P.: Service provision for persons with disabilities – an overview of Hungary in. REER (Revista de Educacao Especial e Reabilitacao) IV. Vol. 21. 2014. Universidade de Lisboa pp. 77 – 89.

RAEVE, L. D. (2014) Paediatric Cochlear Implantation: outcomes and current trends in education and rehabilitation, Netherlands, Ipskamp Drukkers, Enschede, ISBN 978-94-6191-918-2.

The rights of persons with disability or disability rights? (2010) SINOSZ–MDAC–FESZT : Budapest. ISBN 978-963-88487-1-0.

ZÁSZKALICZKY P. – LECHTA, V. – MATUSKA, O. (eds.). New ways of special education – System development, consulting, integration. Eötvös Loránd University Bárczi Gusztáv Faculty of Special Education, Budapest. pp. 315 – 324.

10 The Right to Inclusive Education

10.1 Introduction

Last two decades are strongly influenced by the trend of equalizing of people with and without disabilities. People with disabilities are often discriminated in such basic needs like what to eat, when to get up (Goffman, 1959, in CommDH/IssuePaper (2012)3) and isolated in and with community of disabled people. Artificial creating of borders between human individuals supports prejudices and stereotypes; underestimates some individuals and makes impossible to actualize human beings in (maybe unpredictable) daily-life and leisure activities.

Some scholars have started to mention the right to inclusion, which expresses a right to be a fully valued member of society and the people with disabilities have the right to material and non-material goods, which enable their full participation (Jones, 2011). The UN Convention on the Rights of Person with Disabilities defines *the right to live an independent way of life and the right to be included into society* in Article 19. It is a way of non-discrimination in common elements of human life – work, leisure time, sport, culture, politics and education.

The developed countries have been guarantying the right to education for more than fifty years. This right has usually been fulfilled in dual system of schools – mainstream schools and schools for children with special educational needs (SEN). Experiences with legal adjustment confirm that the dual school system becomes the thing of the past and particular states try to adjust the condition for common education of children with and without SEN. In these days, we should be brave enough to speak about *the right to inclusive education*. Certainly, this term does not have legal support in international or national documents until now. In addition, it contains more questions than answers: Should all pupils with SEN be included in mainstream schools? Why yes/not? Who can teach them? On the other hand, we can see some examples of dealing with an adaptation of inclusive education in national regulation. Following comparison of legal adjustment could help to define and specify *the right to inclusive education* as it is contained in some European countries.

10.2 Comparison on Legal Adjustment

Our comparison embraces countries which academic institutions take part in project researching the quality of life of children with visual or hearing impairment. In the text, we use descriptive and comparative approach. At first, we describe the state *de iure* in Germany, Hungary, Poland and Slovakia and secondly, we compare special care and support of children with hearing and visual impairment.

10.3 Terminus a Quo

The countries, which legal state we mention in this text, historically belong to the countries with dual system of schools – schools for intact children and separated schools for children with disabilities or disorders. For example, the first separated school for deaf pupils in Hungary was established by András Cházár in 1802 in Vác (Tóth 2014). History of care of visual disabled people started in 1825 in Bratislava, where Rafael Beitl taught two blind students and presented their successful study results (Dudeková 2015). After that, the first specialized institution was established in Pest (now Budapest). Tradition of separated schools lasted after World War I (after Austrian-Hungary break-up) and after World War II. Then dual system of schools became the part of legislative norms for education especially in new-formed communist countries.

The change in consideration of education as an essential right of every person together with respect to equal approach and possibilities in education had led to growing effort for legal establishment in which inclusive education of children with sensory disabilities is possible, desired and enforceable. The development of legislative norms was naturally influenced by social and political movements in mentioned countries.

Legal Framework in Bavaria, Germany

In German province *Bavaria,* the education of children with SEN is fulfilled according to the Act on Education (Gesetz über das Erziehungs- und Unterrichtswesen in Bayern, BayEUG) which describes tasks of all school levels. Former regulation, in which the special-education support was task for all levels limited by their possibilities, was changed into requirement: "Inclusive education is task of all school levels" (BayEUG, Art. 2, paragraph 2).

Pupils without and with special education care can be educated in all schools and it is supposed that the mainstream schools are by education of pupils with SEN supported by the special-education authority. Acceptance of pupils with SEN of specified types (visual and hearing impairment, physical and motor development) involves an approval of extra-costs, who can be refused only by significant added costs (BayEUG, Art. 30a/4). Any SENs cannot be the base for affiliation with some certain type of school. The pupils with SEN do not have to reach learning aims in certain grade of schooling in mainstream schools or to fulfil some special conditions. They follow aims set in individual learning plan. If they are not able to reach learning aims in secondary schools and vocational schools, they will receive the certificate with description of reached individual learning aims and recommendation about possibilities of their profession integration and next educational path.

Comparing other described legal norms, the BayEUG is very specific, because it describes educational forms, which help to include the pupils with SEN in mainstream schools in Art. 30a. Cooperative Learning is considered as an appropriate way to improve inclusion. The forms are precisely given:

1. Cooperative Classes where pupils with and without SEN are educated together. The pupils with SEN are supported by Mobile Special Education Service at lessons.
2. Partner Classes is based on the cooperation of mainstream school class and special school class, which create the mutual and regular lessons during which the learning aims are distinguished.
3. Open Classes of Special Schools, in which the pupils with SEN are educated according to learning plans of mainstream schools. Special schools have to be able to provide this type of education without next personal or space needs. According to Article 30b in BayEUG, the inclusive school is a development aim of all schools. It is supposed that the pupils with SEN, who attend the mainstream schools, are educated respecting their special needs and they are supported by the Mobile Special Education Service. The mainstream schools can develop the school profile "Inclusion" if the local school authority gives the permission. In these schools, the common concept of education is followed considering individual requests (in Art. 41 and Art. 30a). The educational forms are adapted to all pupils' educational needs (with or without SEN). Orienta-

tion on the school profile "Inclusion" integrates the condition of enlarging the school staff by special educators. The special educators giving advice to mainstream teachers and pupils with SEN are responsible for diagnosing special needs and teaching in classroom with pupils with and without SEN. The mainstream schools and special schools change educational experiences as was mentioned in text above. The school with the school profile "Inclusion" can be grounded also for children with more complex special needs and it works in system of mainstream school with mixed classes. Again – the support of school staff by special educators is needed and the classes in those schools have to be permitted by the authority accepting special costs.

In Bavaria, the system of special schools for pupils with hearing and visual impairment is preserved and the regions have a legal obligation to retain these schools (Art. 33, BayEUG). If there is a non-government or a private organization, which provides special education for pupils and educates according to state curriculum, mentioned obligation do not have to be fulfilled.

The special school supportive centres are built for public:

1. Supportive centres focused on visual, hearing, body and motor development, centres for language development (for grades 7 – 9, secondary schools – grade 10, vocational schools).
2. Supportive centres focused on language, learning and social and emotional development including built special educational supportive centres, supportive centres aimed on mental development and schools for ill children.

Both types of centres mentioned above can be built in certain district or built for smaller districts as common centres.

The pupils with SEN fulfil their obligatory school attendance in mainstream schools or special schools. They can attend the special schools only in the case that they need certain special care. The choice of the school depends on decision of pupils' legal representatives. When the pupils are in adult age, they choose – having appropriate ability to decide – their school alone. Pupils' legal representatives are supposed to inform about possible schools in advance and they can ask for advice by Mobile Special-education Service or Youth Help. To be enrolled for special school, the special education expertise is needed.

According to Art 41, BayEUG, the pupils with SEN do not have to be enrolled at mainstream school or school with profile "Inclusion", when the development of included pupil is endangered or he/she threatens the rights of other pupils seriously.

Legal Framework in Hungary

Similar changes can be found in development of legal state in *Hungary*. As Tóth (2014, p. 2) writes the Act of 1993 (LXXIX) was determinative from the perspective of special education and "different groups of disabilities (such as sensory disability, physical disability, speaking disability, mental disability, autism and 'other disabilities') were categorised in term 'disability', which was consequently used instead of 'special needs'".

The Public School Act defines right of every child to receive education and teaching at the institutions of public education and to receive services of an identical standard on identical conditions to other persons being in a comparable position on the basis of the requirement of equal treatment (Article A/4). Of course, also other rights connected with education are guaranteed, such as right to be educated and taught in safety and healthy environment and have a daily routine formed by building periods of rest, leisure and physical exercise in and by giving opportunities for sport and eating in compliance with their age and stage of development. The personality, human dignity and rights of a child shall be respected and protection has to be provided for them against physical and mental violence; children may not be subject to corporal punishment, torture or cruel and humiliating retribution or treatment.

In that Act, the definition of children/pupils with SEN can be found. Csépé (2008, in Tóth, 2014) distinguishes two categories of SEN according to amendment from 2007 – 'SEN-a' means a pupil's SEN are traced back to organic causes while symptoms of 'SEN-b' group are not. Using legal description to make it clearer: SEN-a group embraces pupils with physical, organoleptic, mental or lalopathic disabilities, autistic children; they are multi-disabled in case of the simultaneous occurrence of several disabilities; those who struggle with the chronic and serious derangement of cognitive functions and the development of behaviour ascribable to organic reasons. SEN-b group embraces pupils struggling with the chronic and serious derangement of cognitive functions and of the development of behaviour not ascribable to organic reasons according to the expert opinion of the rehabilitation committee of experts.

However, The Public School Act mentions also the category of so-called disadvantaged pupils – whose entitlement to a regular child protection allowance on the basis of their social background established by the public administration officer. Multi-disadvantaged child is child taken into long-term foster care or children whose parents exercising the statutory control over them in accordance with their voluntary statement made in the course of the procedure by the Act on Child Protection. Legal regulation in Hungary ensures that students with learning disabilities or mild mental disabilities do not have to go to special schools or classes since 2003 (Tóth, 2014).

According to Article 30, pupils with SEN have the right to receive pedagogical, therapeutic educational, conductive educational service corresponding to their condition within the scope of special care after their legitimate claim has been established. Special care shall be provided within school education depending on the age and condition of the child and is connected with expert opinion of the rehabilitation committees of experts. To fulfil the conditions of special care, school classes with differentiated curricula can be formed. School education and teaching of pupils have to be established in compliance with the type of the disability, identically with the therapeutic educational-teaching institution.

If a pupil struggles with adaptive, learning or behavioural difficulties or with the chronic and serious derangement of cognitive functions and the development of behaviour ascribable to organic reasons, they are entitled to developmental education, which may be realised within the scope of educational counselling, kindergarten education, school education and teaching, hall of residence education and teaching. Pupils with SEN are exempted from evaluation and assessment in certain subjects or parts of subjects by the head teacher, with the exception of practical training, according to the expert opinion of the rehabilitation committee of experts or the educational counselling service in accordance with the division of labour as prescribed by statute. If a student is exempted from evaluation and assessment in certain subjects or parts of subjects, the school organises individual activities for them and helps the student to catch up with the others within the scope of the individual activities based on an individual development plan. When students are tested in a written form, they have to be allowed of the employment of the aid (typewriter, computer etc.) employed in the course of their school studies or, if necessary, the substitution of written testing with oral testing or oral testing with written testing.

Educational institution is bound with duty to create appropriate necessary conditions for the education and teaching of pupils with SEN. That means according to legal definition: employment of conductive therapists and therapeutic teachers in compliance with the separate kindergarten education or school education and teaching of pupils and the type and severity of the special educational need, application of a special curriculum, textbooks or any other special aids necessary for education and teaching; engagement of therapeutic teachers with qualifications in a special field necessary for private tuition, integrated kindergarten education, school education and teaching, developmental preparation and activities specified by the competent committee of experts; a special curriculum, textbooks and special therapeutic and technical tools necessary for the activities; provision of the professional services specified by the rehabilitation committee of experts for pupils.

Legal Framework in Poland

To describe the legal framework in *Poland*, we should start with regulations contained in the Polish Constitution, in which discrimination on any ground is prohibited. Public authorities are obligated to ensure special health care to children and persons with disabilities and to assist to persons with disabilities to ensure their subsistence, and facilitate their adaptation to work and social communication (Art. 68 – 69). According to Article 72, the most important children's right are guaranteed by ensuring protection of the rights of the child and "everyone shall have the right to demand of organs of public authority that they defend children against violence, cruelty, exploitation and depravity".

The main legal framework for inclusive education is contained in the Act on the Education System (Ustawa z 7 września 1991 r. o systemie oświaty, with further amendments). Under the Act children with disabilities are entitled to (Art. 1): education in all types of schools according to their individual needs and predisposition; changes of the content, methods and organisation of the education according to their SEN; possibilities to use special forms of teaching and psychological and education support, realisation of individual educational plan and rehabilitation activities, prolongation of every stage of education, assessment of their knowledge and qualifications in adapted forms and conditions, free accommodation in a special educational-pedagogical centre, free transport and assistance to school or special centre.

In Polish educational system, a recognition of the need for special organisation of education is done by a public guidance and counselling centre. Children with SEN are supposed to obtain broad specialist support during their education, adjusted learning conditions and, in some cases, also adapted curriculum. Despite of supporting integration/inclusion of children with SEN in mainstream schools, in Poland exist also special school for children with certain type of disability.

The group of pupils with SEN embraces various types of disabilities as follows: physical disability, intellectual disability, blind and visually impaired, deaf and hearing impaired, autistic children and children with Asperger syndrome, multiple impairments, abnormal social functioning (who need rehabilitation or/and social therapy).

Schooling of those pupils is realized in different types of schools: a) mainstream schools can provide inclusive education (pupils with SEN are in mainstream classes), b) mainstream schools which offer education for pupils with SEN in special classes (pupils with SEN do not take part in education in mainstream classes), c) integrative classes in mainstream schools or integrative schools (where all classes are integrative classes), d) special schools and residential special schools.

Following amendments (2010) brought the changes into SEN pupil education. Attention is paid on better access to early support, early intervention and pre-school education; flexible model of education respecting SEN; improving quality of teaching methods; taking in account the nature of the disability by forms and conditions of external exams.

In special schools, only some pupils with SEN are educated. Traditionally, there are schools for blind and visually impaired students, deaf and hearing impaired students, students with learning disabilities, students with physical and multiple disabilities and students with autism. Legal representatives of children with SEN are allowed to request their including in mainstream schools (Art. 71b). Legal regulation obliges special residential schools to co-operate and support mainstream schools. Special schools can help to solve educational problems of students with disabilities. Unfortunately, no certain conditions and rules defining this co-operation are defined.

On the other hand, headmasters of the mainstream schools are responsible for forms of support. They create conditions to support:

a) Specialist classes, i.e. correctional-compensatory classes (students with specific learning difficulties or other developmental dysfunctions); social, speech therapy; psychological therapy.
b) Compensatory classes for pupils with learning difficulties.
c) Activities developing talents for gifted children.
d) Therapeutic classes for students who require adaptation of the learning process to their specific learning needs and long-term specialist support. These classes are in mainstream integrative schools.

Legal Framework in Slovakia

To outline the situation *in Slovakia*, some changes in legislation since 1984 are discussed. In Slovakia (in 1984 part of Czechoslovakia), the dual system of schools was supported by School Act 29/1984 Zb. in which the special schools were called as schools for youth with special care. It should be said that three kinds of special schools are mentioned:

1. The special schools for youth involving special care intended for pupils with auditory disability, sensual disability, pupils with speech impediment, pupils with physical disability, difficult-educable pupils and for ill and enfeebled pupils in medical institutions. It was supposed that the curriculum of those pupils is comparable with the curriculum of intact children and their education is equal (§ 29).
2. The special schools for pupils with some mental disabilities that make impossible to educate them successfully in mainstream schools or special schools for youth with special care (§ 31). Pupils were educated according to the level of their mental ability. The School Act used two terms – pupils mentally advanced and pupils mentally retarded.
3. The remedial schools (§33) for hard-educable pupils with lack of mental development, which makes impossible education in special schools, but they are educable. Their curriculum was focused on basic habits of hygiene, appropriate knowledge and work skills with daily-used objects/ tools.

According to Act 29/1984 Zb., the extra-conditions and interest were legally guaranteed for pupils with outstanding talent (nowadays gifted pupils). The classes with extended curriculum were founded in some schools. The gifted pupils were allowed to finish their compulsory school attendance earlier than other students were and individual form of studying was possible. It can be briefly said that these conditions are still maintained.

Significant changes in legal adjustment towards pupils with special care came into practice as natural consequences after social and political turn in 1989. In amendment from 1990, the right of deaf and sightless people on education in their language was finally guaranteed – using sign language and Braille (§ 2). Official name for schools for youth with special care was changed on "Special schools". Next important changes were brought by amendment 229/2000 Z. z., the term pupil with special educational need (SEN) was introduced and also the names for special schools for children with mental disabilities were changed respecting political correctness (previous names carried negative, degradable connotations).

Revised Act 29/1984 Zb. emphasized the significance of appropriate care for pupils with disabilities – the article about them was completed into §3. (Pupils with mental, auditory, visual or physical disability, ill and enfeebled pupils, pupils with impaired communication skills, pupils with autism, pupils with developmental learning or behaviour disorders, pupils with severe mental disability placed in social services homes, pupils with psychical or social development disorders, the education corresponding their individual skills is provided by special form and methods according to their disability.)

To support better school results of children from social disadvantaged environment, the possibility to form so-called "the zero grade" in mainstream grammar schools was introduced in 2002 (Amendment 408/2002). The education in that degree is oriented on acceleratory programmes and exercises improving cognitive and non-cognitive functions. The pupils, who have not reached the school maturity, come from social disadvantaged environment and are not able to master the first degree, are allowed to attend the zero degree. In the same amendment, the profession of teacher assistant was introduced legally. Teacher assistants could work in mainstream schools and in special schools.

Amendment 365/2004 Z. z. brought extensive adjustment of school integration into original act. At first, the right to non-discriminative approach was introduced – the rights contained in act are guaranteed to all applicants and pupils; discrimination because of sex, religion, marital and family status, colour, language, political thoughts, professional activities, national or social origin, health disability, age, property was forbidden. Schools were not allowed to favourite or disadvantage the pupils who used the rights according to act.

Definition and forms of school integration were set in new §32a. Integration was considered as education of pupils with SEN, except pupils educated in classes of special schools. Forms of integration were defined as:

a) Integration in special classes, which are part of mainstream grammar or secondary school. The part of education can be realized with other pupils in school and the education is realized by teacher from both classes (special and intact). Pupil from special class can attend some school subjects out of special class. Special classes are usually formed for pupils with SEN with the same kind of disability.

b) Individual integration – pupils with SEN are integrated in mainstream classes and are educated according to individual educational programme (IEP). The curriculum and teaching methodology are adapted to their needs.

Integrated pupil is pupil with SEN who was gained to school on the grounds of written expertise of institution for special education consulting after diagnostic examination. The act made the headmasters responsible for acceptance of pupils with SEN and for guaranteeing necessary technical, material, expert and personal conditions, e. g. classroom setting and equipment, compensatory tools. They should ensure that in the case of integrated pupils the demands are not lower and comply with their possibilities. Assessment and evaluation of pupils with SEN follow pupils' possibilities. The class/form teacher started to be responsible for individual educational programmes of pupils with SEN. IEP should be drawn up in cooperation with special education consultants.

The new organization of integration of pupils with SEN required setting of rights and duties for all participants – intact pupils, pupils with SEN, parents and teachers (§ 32c). Pupils with SEN has right on individual approach in education respecting his/her abilities and state of health, to be educated by teacher with expert and professional qualification, to be educated in safety and health environment, on respect to his/her personality and on protection against physical and mental violence. Realization of integrated pupil rights cannot be limited rights of other participants in educational process. Legal representatives (usually parents) regularly consult educational results with form teacher, with school special teacher or institution for special education consulting.

In 2008, the previous Act 29/1984 Zb. was completely substituted by new School Act 245/2008 Z. z. However, the new adjustment did not bring principal changes in setting of inclusive education. Pupils with SEN are divided into few groups – e.g. with health disability, with developmental disorders, gifted pupils etc. (§ 1). Only school integration is declared in the School Act (it is considered as education of pupils with SEN in school classes, which are set for intact pupils). The principle of prohibition of all forms of discrimination, especially segregation, and equal access to education with respect to individual educational needs and co-responsibility for own education are stated in § 2. In mainstream schools, the specialised class can be built. In specialised classes, the pupils who do not have predisposition to master content of curriculum of certain grade can be educated. Pupils with SEN are educated in specialised classroom in necessary needed time, after that, they come back to previous class.

10.4 Comparison on Inclusion of Pupils with Visual and Hearing Impairment

As was shown in our previous text, compared countries are very similar in more aspects. In the case of pupils with visual or hearing impairment, the dual system of schools exists in given countries. Legal representatives of these pupils are allowed to decide if their child is going to be educated in mainstream or special schools. If they are educated in mainstream schools, the regulation usually guarantee some compensatory help or guidance how to make education of pupils with visual or hearing impairments more successful.

In Slovakia pupils with visual or/and hearing impairment are considered as pupils with health disability according to the School Act 245/2008 Z. z. If they are integrated in mainstream school, the school has a legitimate claim to special foundation from state. According to §13 schoolbooks in Braille approved by Ministry of Education are given to schools in which education is considered as systematic preparation for next vocation. Pupils, who were included into mainstream kindergartens or schools, can be moved to another school, if headmaster found out that education of pupil with SEN is not to his/her profit or to profit of other children taking part in education (§28, §29). If legal representatives of child do not agree with redeployment, the court will decide about the place of child's next education. Pupils with visual or hearing impairments can be supported by help of teaching assistant at lessons (schools may ask local school authority for founding teaching assistant's position). In Slovak legal system, the pupils with serious disability can have a personal assistant who helps with mobility and orientation, self-service and communication (447/2008 Z. z.). The personal assistants are not usually supposed to assist at lessons at school. Need for pupil's personal assistant who takes care of pupil and help him/ her to master school tasks is accomplished only in extra cases with regard to circumstances. If the school cannot guarantee safety and health protection of pupil with SEN or other children at class; or there are so barriers (e.g. problem with communication pupil-teacher) which pupil cannot overcome without help because of his/her disability, the personal assistance should be supported. It should be highlighted that personal assistant or teaching assistant are very often only people who can make easier pupils' inclusion. The schools are not obligated to create a position of special teacher at school; it is only possibility. Unfortunately, proclaimed help of special assistant centres is usually (if not always) limited on special examination and expert opinions, their real support of pupil in classroom reality is missing.

As we mentioned, the children with visual or/and hearing impairment can be educated in mainstream or integrative schools in Poland. The Minister of National Education is obligated to co-fund manuals and schoolbooks for these pupils according the Education Act. To improve process of integration, the number of pupils is changed and some extra activities are offered. Kulesza (2016) mentions rules in mainstream schools – one or two children with SEN can be in a group/classroom, maximal number of children is thirty, children are supported by specialist activities in counselling centres. In integrative schools, the maximal number of pupils is twenty, maximal number of pupils with SEN is three to five (proportion: one child with SEN to four children without SEN). The teacher with qualification in special education is employed in these types of classes; resource room for additional activities is used. Integrative classes are extra funded from the state budget.

In Bavaria, Germany, the situation of school inclusion conditions is similar to Poland. Legal representatives decide, in which school the pupil with SEN will be educated. In the case of hearing or/and visual impairment, the child can be educated in special schools or in mainstream schools. The pupil with SEN can be educated in school with orientation on the school profile "Inclusion". "Inclusive" schools are obligated to have enlarged school staff – special educators. It can be supposed, that in inclusive school conditions, the children with hearing or/and visual impairment have unique possibilities for development within their schoolmates without SEN. As we mentioned, the pupils with SEN do not have to be enrolled at mainstream school or school with profile "Inclusion" or can be expelled, when the development of included pupil is endangered or he/she threatens the rights of other pupils seriously.

In Hungarian school system, pupils with hearing and/or visual impairment can be included in mainstream education. One of the compensatory tools is change of the number of pupils in class. Pupils with SEN are regarding as two or three depending on the type of disability, pupils with hearing/visual impairment are regarded as three people. For pupils with SEN, compulsory health and rehabilitation class activities are organised.

10.5 Conclusion

After description legal framework in Bavaria in Germany, Poland, Hungary and Slovakia, we may summarise main features of adjustment of the right to inclusive education in state regulations. Development from strict dual systems of schools to dual systems of schools in which education of all children in mainstream schools is preferred rather than their segregation into special schools is typical feature connecting compared countries. However, the quality of fulfilment of this right varies according to country. Firstly, it seems to be progressive to create conditions for so-called integrative or inclusive classroom or schools, in which process of inclusion is strongly supported by personal and expert capacity. This approach is represented in regulations, that oblige state and school fund the capacities of special educators and special counselling, integrative or special education centres. Secondly, some of the compared regulations also express exactly what curriculum and individual education plan should be expected; and put stress on fact that the pupils with SEN do not have to master the same curriculum content as pupils without SEN. Thirdly, the regulations do not make absolute the right to inclusive education. Similarly like the right to education, in which right to be educated in some schools and for some profession is limited by mental and physical predispositions, the right to inclusive education is limited by two restrictions: 1. Pupils with SEN can be moved from schools, if they do not benefit from schooling or/and 2. Pupils with SEN can be expelled from schools, if their attendance endangered other pupils at schools or classrooms. Certainly, the third point would require legal specification in compared regulations not to be exploited.

Literature

Act No. LXXIX of 1993 on Public Education. [on line] [cited 10-10-2016]. Available on http://www.nefmi.gov.hu/letolt/english/act_lxxxix_1993_091103.pdf.

Bayerisches Gesetz über das Erziehungs- und Unterrichtswesen (BayEUG) in der Fassung der Bekanntmachung vom 31. Mai 2000 (GVBl. p. 414, ber. p. 632) BayRS 2230-1-1-K [on line] [cited 10-11-2016]. Available on http://www.gesetze-bayern.de/Content/Document/BayEUG.

CommDH/IssuePaper (2012) 3 The Right of People with Disabilites to Live Independently and Be Included in the Community. [on line] [cited 10-07-2016]. Available on: https://wcd.coe.int/ViewDoc.jsp?id=1917847.

DUDEKOVÁ, G. (2015) Humanizácia starostlivosti o hendikepovaných. Telesne a duševne postihnutí na prahu modernej doby. In História. Revue o dejinách spoločnosti, Vol. 13, № 3 – 4/2015. [on line] [cited 10-10-2016]. Available on http://www.historiarevue.sk/index.php?id=2005dudekova5.

JONES, M. (2011) Inclusion, Social Inclusion and Participation. In RIOUX, M. H. – BASER, L. A. – JONES, M. Critical Perspectives on Human Rights and Disability Law. Leiden: Martinus Nijhoff Publisher and VSP, pp. 57 – 87.

KULESZA, E. M. – VALEEVA, R. A. (2016) Education for Persons with Special Needs: Polish and Russian Experience. In *International Journal of Environmental & Science Education*, 2016, Vol. 11, № 7, pp. 1619 – 1629.

TÓTH, A. N. (2014) Theory and Practice of Inclusive Education in Hungary. In *Electronic Journal for Inclusive Education*, Vol. 3, № 2 (Summer/Fall 2014). [on line] [cited 10-10-2016]. Available on http://corescholar.libraries.wright.edu/ cgi/viewcontent. cgi?article=1162&context=ejie.

Ustawa z 7 września 1991 r. o systemie oświaty [on line] [cited 10-11-2016]. Available on https://www.portaloswiatowy.pl/wspolpraca-szkoly-z-organami/ustawa-z-7-wrzesnia-1991-r.-o-systemie-oswiaty-tekst-jedn.-dz.u.-z-2015-poz.-2156-10023.html.

Zákon č. 245/2008 Z. z. o výchove a vzdelávaní (Školský zákon).

Zákon č. 447/2008 Z. z. o peňažných príspevkoch na kompenzáciu ťažkého zdravotného postihnutia a o zmene a doplnení niektorých zákonov.

Directory

Miroslava Bartoňová – professor at the Department of Special Education, Faculty of Education, Charles University, Prague. Her main scientific interests are focused on education and approaches towards students with specific learning difficulties and with intellectual disabilities. She also focuses on didactics of teaching students with special educational needs.
E-mail: miroslava.bartonova@pedf.cuni.cz

Naďa Bizová – assistant professor at the Department of Education Studies, Faculty of Education, Trnava University in Slovakia. She is focused on the field of leisure time education, inclusive education and theory of education.
E-mail: nada.bizova@truni.sk

Jaroslava Gajdošíková Zeleiová – associate professor at the Department of Educational Studies, Faculty of Education, Trnava University in Slovakia, forensic expert in clinical pedopsychology and psychology. Field of professional interest: music therapy, psychodynamics and sociodynamics.
E-mail: klinicka.psychologia@gmail.com

Grażyna Gunia – associate professor and head of the Department of Speech-language Pathology at the Institute of Special Education, Pedagogical University, Krakow. Specialization: special education, rehabilitation of deaf and hearing impairedhearing impaired person, speech therapy. Her scientific and research focus is on revalidation of the hearing impaired and the hard-of-hearing, speech therapy, health education.
E-mail: gragun@up.krakow.pl

Joanna Konarska – professor of the Department of Psychology and Humanities of Andrzej Frycz Modrzewski Krakow University. She is a professional psychologist with a specialization in child clinical psychology and educational psychology, with a more than 30 years of experience in comprehensive rehabilitation of people with visual disabilities in their natural environment. Research objectives are determined by the practical knowledge of visual disability in the context of specific visual disability on background problems common to all people with disabilities.
E-mail: jokona@akon.pl

Viktor Lechta – professor of the pedagogy and special pedagogy. He is focused on diagnostic and therapy of persons with communicative disability, history of the care for persons with disabilities and inclusive education.
E-mail: vlechta@gmail.com

Annette Leonhardt – dean of the Faculty of Psychology and Educational Sciences, holds the chair of Education for the Deaf and Hearing Impaired at the Ludwig Maximilians University of Munich. Since 1999 her research activities have focused on the inclusion of hearing impaired children and adolescents and the provision of CI for deaf children of deaf parents. She has initiated numerous international collaborations and research projects, e. g. with Japan, Slovakia and Ethiopia.
E-mail: leonhardt@edu.lmu.de

Eva Lörinczová – teacher, Doctor of Philosophy in Education, graduate from Constantine the Philosopher University in Nitra, Slovakia. Fields of her professional interest: theory of education, inclusive education, social interaction of students with SEN in inclusive settings.
Email: eva.lorinczova@ukf.sk

Andrea Perlusz – Vice-Dean at the Faculty of Therapeutic Education of G. Bárczi at the Eötvös Loránd University in Budapest and head of the Department of Hearing Impaired Education at the above mentioned faculty. Key fields of interest: inclusive education of children and pupils with special education needs, possibilities of parents' involvement, integrated education and education of children with hearing disabilities.
E-mail: perlusz.andrea@barczi.elte.hu

Anna Sádovská – assistant professor at the Department of Educational Studies, Faculty of Education, Trnava University, Slovakia. Her work is focused on ethical and legal principles asserted in inclusive education.
E-mail: anna.sadovska@gmail.com

Marie Vítková – professor and head of the Department of Special Education, Faculty of Education at Masaryk University, Brno. Scientific and research activities: special education, inclusive education, education of students with physical disabilities and multiple impairments.
E-mail: vitkova@ped.muni.cz

Erik Žovinec – associate professor at the Faculty of Education, Constantine Philosopher University in Nitra. He is author and supervisor of study program Special Education and Education of persons with Specific Learning Disability at CPU in Nitra. Field of his professional interest: inclusive education, dyslexia testing, remediation, therapy and counselling SLD children and students.
E-mail: ezovinec@ukf.sk

www.ingramcontent.com/pod-product-compliance
Lightning Source LLC
LaVergne TN
LVHW052128070326
832902LV00039B/4226